KEEPING UP WITH THE COMPETITION

Learn What Your Top Competitors
Are Doing for Success in Online Marketing

Gini Graham Scott, PhD

KEEPING UP WITH THE COMPETITION

TABLE OF CONTENTS

INTRODUCTION

No matter what industry you are in or what kind of products and services you offer, a key to success is knowing what the competition is doing so you can better compete. This is especially true in the new digital economy. Now there are various tools for learning what your competitors are doing - from looking at the products and services they are offering to learning about their packaging, pricing, and promotional activities.

These products can include anything, including physical and digital products, print and e-books, and in-person and online services, such as coaching, consulting, and training in any field. The emphasis in this book is on online and digital products and services and on online tools and techniques for learning about these offerings, though these techniques can apply to physical products and in-person services, too.

In the digital world, because of the importance of websites and online sales platforms, this competitor intel can include knowing the keywords and tools they are using on their website, and where and how they are advertising. This information can help you determine what techniques work best, as well as determine the sites where and how they are advertising, so you can create your own ads on these sites or in other media. For example, this effort can lead you to other marketplaces, including the social media, to promote your own products and services.

In effect, you want to explore what your competitors has been doing to achieve their success, so you can apply and adapt that model to your own marketing efforts, which will help you become more successful.

You obviously don't want to come up with a me-too product, where you generally can only compete on price if you can offer your own products and services to the same market. Rather, your goal should be to come up with a product or service that you can promote as being different and better. By understanding your competition you can better decide what changes or modifications you might make or what new and unique products or services you can offer to appeal to that market.

Once you have an idea or have already created a book, product, or service, you can see what the most successful individuals or companies with a similar idea or project have done. The first step is to find who they are in their major markets for sales. Then, you can learn more about them and what they have done to achieve success. In effect, you are reverse engineering a successful business, so you model your website and marketing strategy based on what has worked for your competitors.

The two major markets are Amazon and Click Bank. In both cases, you want to do a search based on the name or topic of a book or on the terms describing a product or service. Then, look at the results and determine the highest ranking books, products or services. I'll use books, health and fitness products, and an online course which opens the door for consulting, coaching, and other services to illustrate.

Additionally, to optimize your website, you can learn ways to do this by analyzing your competitors' websites. Plus you get obtain leads and links which you can use in your own marketing efforts. So the book features some tools to help you conduct this analysis.

The following chapters will guide you through a variety of methods you can use to learn about your competition in order to guide our own product development and marketing strategy. The book includes illustrations to help you understand what to do.

CHAPTER 1: FINDING COMPETITORS ON AMAZON

You can conduct a search directly on Amazon, or if you have a book, you can use a tool called PublisherRocket (originally called KDP Rocket) that will help to speed up your search, as well as provide you with additional insights about other books in your field on Amazon.

Searching for Competitors on Amazon

To find competitors on Amazon, use the search field to find authors with similar books or companies with similar products. Look at the top 5 to 7 items in the field, and drill down by looking at each listing to see the categories they are listed in. Make a note of those categories, because you initially get 2 or 3 categories, but you can call Amazon support to ask for up to 10 categories. List as many categories as you can, because when customers do a search and use that category, they may find your book or product.

For example, say you have a diet or fitness book or product, which is a popular category. You might try a search with a series of terms: "diet…nutrition…food…weight loss…wellness…good health." If you put in "diet" for all categories, you will see the first rows with sponsored products, including a Pepsi pitch, some pills, and a plan.

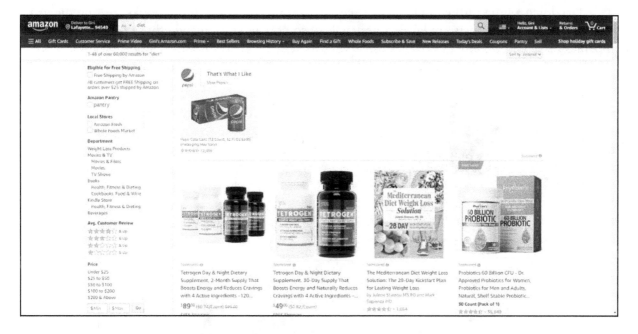

The next rows, based on organic search for the most popular products will show other diet pills and medications, as well as a couple of books on the topic.

Go down a little further and you can see even more variety and more books. Along the way, you'll see that some products are labeled best sellers, so you want to include those on the list of top competitors in your category.

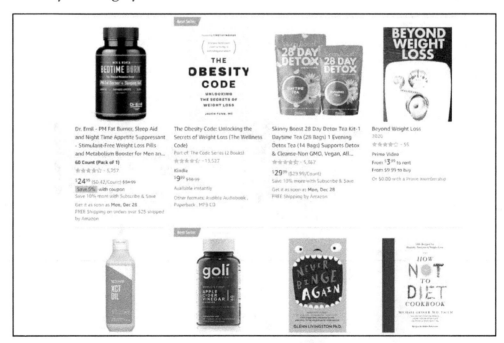

Notice the reviews, too. You'll notice that the top competitors have 4 to 5 star reviews. This is important, since you want to model your marketing approach after those products with good reviews of at least 4 stars.

You also want to zero in more precisely on your type of product to see your top competitors. One way to do this is by putting a more descriptive listing of your product in the search field, such as limiting your search to "diet plans" rather than the broader term: "diet."

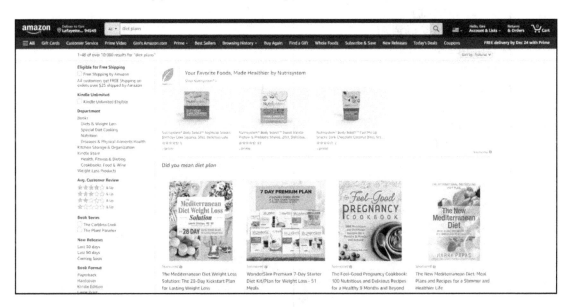

You can limit your search even further by selecting a particular category. Just click the "All" button in the search field to see a drop down menu listing the different sales categories on Amazon.

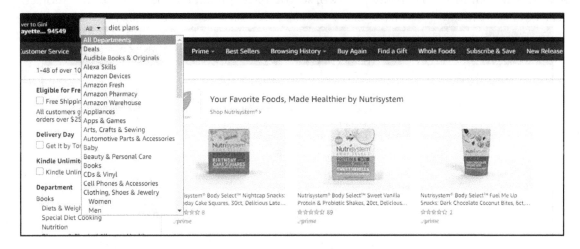

Here are even more categories to choose from:

Say you want to create a course on the subject. You'll see the available products are narrowed down even more. There are just two, so you have limited competition on that subject.

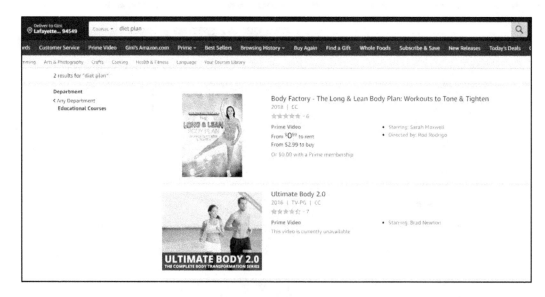

If you want to expand the topic, say to "diet" generally, you'll see many more courses, which are available as software or on video, indicating the format to use for presenting your own course.

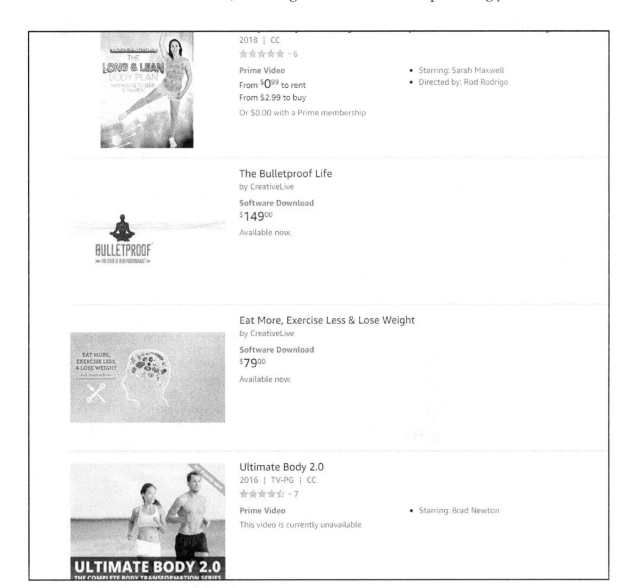

2018 | CC
⭐⭐⭐⭐⭐ ⌄ 6

Prime Video
From $0⁹⁹ to rent
From $2.99 to buy
Or $0.00 with a Prime membership

- Starring: Sarah Maxwell
- Directed by: Rod Rodrigo

The Bulletproof Life
by CreativeLive

Software Download
$149⁰⁰
Available now.

Eat More, Exercise Less & Lose Weight
by CreativeLive

Software Download
$79⁰⁰
Available now.

Ultimate Body 2.0
2016 | TV-PG | CC
⭐⭐⭐⭐½ ⌄ 7

Prime Video
This video is currently unavailable

- Starring: Brad Newton

Or say you have a book. A huge number of items are listed, first the books available on Amazon Prime, then the sponsored books, and finally others based on their popularity.

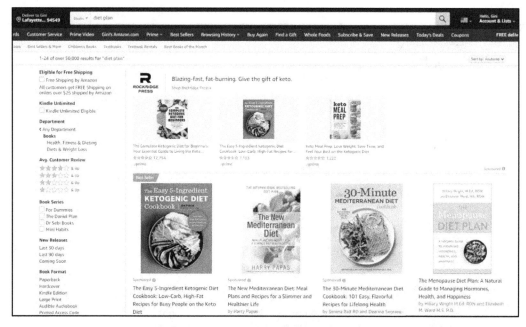

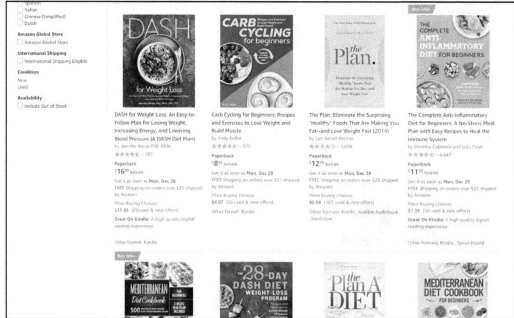

Anyway, you get the idea. Whether you have a book, course, product, or service turned into a product you can sell, you want to see what other competitors are in that market.

Examining the Listings More Closely

To further drill down on what your competitors are doing, look more closely at those items that are not sponsored or listed on Amazon Prime, since this will give you a better idea of the most popular items in your field based on their organic listings.

Some of the things to look at are pricing to see the common range of prices -- such as $9 to $15 for most of these books -- and the number of reviews - with the most popular ones having several hundred to several thousand reviews. You can increase your sales chances if you can price your product in this range, preferably at the lower end, since you will have a new product entry. You can't do much about competing against a large number of reviews when you are first starting. But you can complete by offering special incentives to buy and try now, such as offering a free gift to those who like your product and post a favorable review.

Additionally, consider the look of the packaging, which is especially important if you are selling a book, plan, course, or software. The book cover has to effectively illustrate the message or content you are offering, whereas the package for a product usually has to show the product up close or being used.

If you are creating the cover, take into consideration the look and feel of the covers of the 5 to 7 top selling competitors and incorporate them into your own design, or send the images in a PDF, JPG, or Word document to the designer to use as a guide to creating a new design for you. For example, in the above series of popular books on diet plans, most of the books feature a close-up of some food or a plate of food, so you probably want to include that element in your book.

When you drill down even further to look at the particular top selling items, you will see more details about the product, including the key benefits it is offering. This copy might give you some ideas on writing the copy for your own item, though change the wording. You will also see the different ways the product is available, such as both a paperback and a Kindle e-book, with a special free purchase for those with Kindle Unlimited.

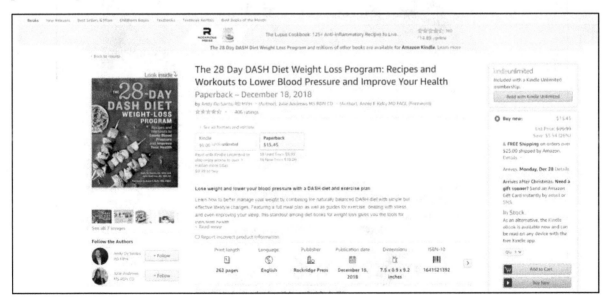

In addition, you'll see what customers also viewed and the sponsored products related to this item, which can give you more ideas about your competitors in this niche.

In many cases, you'll see additional promotional information from the company, which can give you ideas on how to promote your own item.

If there are reviews from editorial or professional reviewers, you can see those, too. Importantly, you can see details about the product, including the publisher or company selling it, a physical description of the item, and the categories where it is listed. Generally, these will be categories you want to be in as well. As you look at more of these details for different books or products, you can add other categories, or notice which categories are listed the most, so you can appear in the ten most frequently listed categories.

If there are any promotional or informational videos related to an item, there will be links to them, and there may be even more about the book authors or product developers. You can similarly add videos and additional author information to your own book or product descriptions.

Amazon also features other products related to this item.

Additionally, you can see customer reviews, including any photos posted by customers about the product, such as these photos of food dishes. These reviews can go on for pages and pages if there are a lot of reviews -- at the end of one page you just click to see more. There is also a graph showing the percentage of reviewers who gave the product 1 to 5 stars.

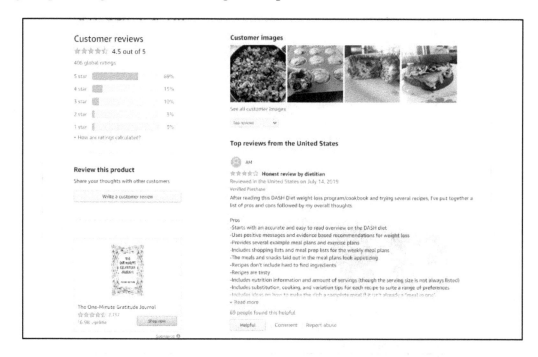

Finally, Amazon indicates the products that customers of this product also bought or viewed -- which are often the same items in both categories.

Amazon is posting all of this information to encourage buyers of one product to buy even more related products. But you can also use it to look at the top products and get insights to apply in packaging and promoting your own product.

Physical products are treated in a similar way. For example, say your product is the line of containers that accompany a food plan.

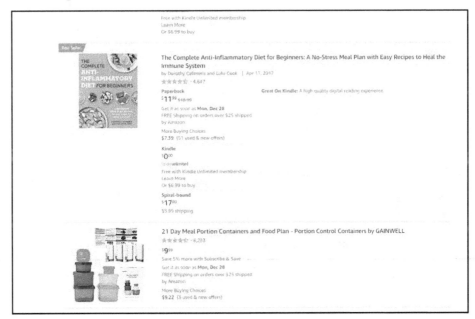

You will see the product and its packaging, along with details on how you can get it.

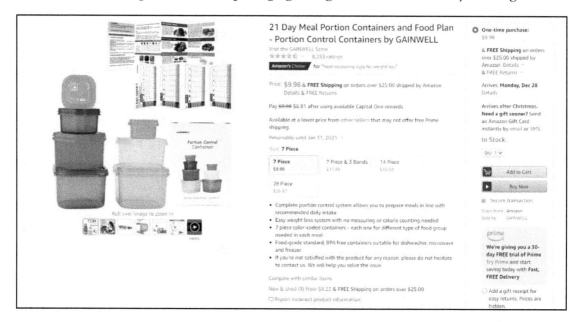

In addition, as with books, you will see examples of other related frequently bought items, along with examples of related products with especially high ratings of 4 stars or more.

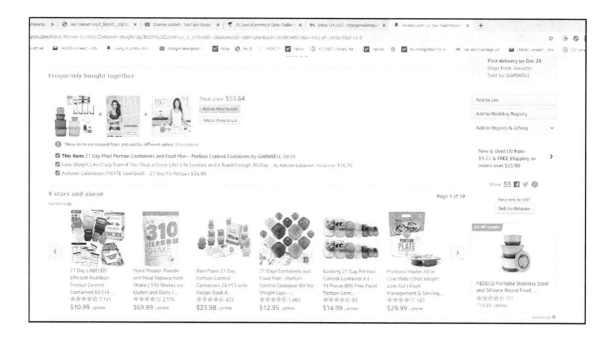

Then, much like the detailed description of the book, you will see more information about the product.

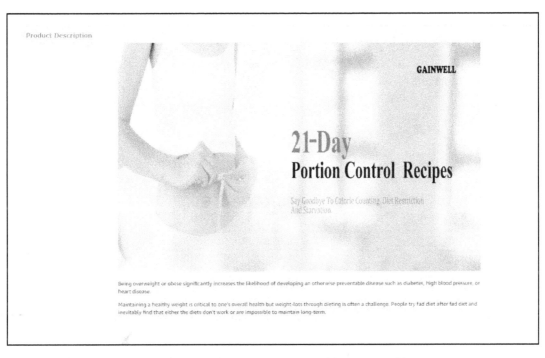

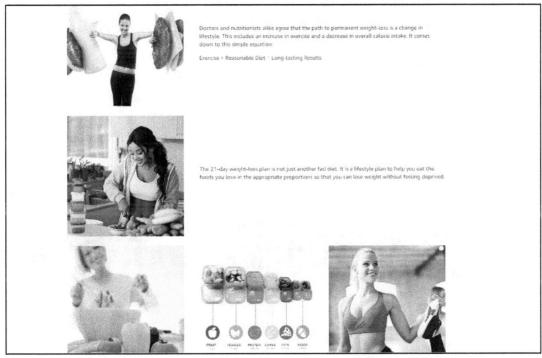

There's a comparison with other similar products, with an opportunity to buy those, too.

Then, there's even more detailed product information, plus some promotional videos.

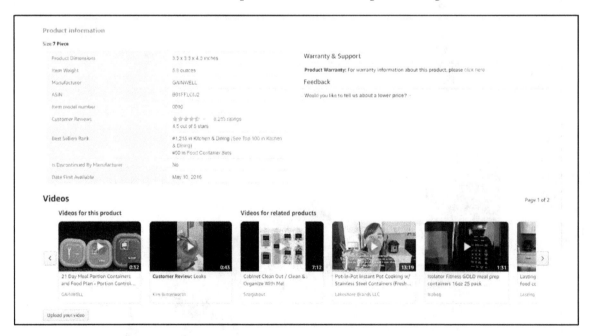

Again, Amazon features more similar products.

After that there's a section for customer questions and answers.

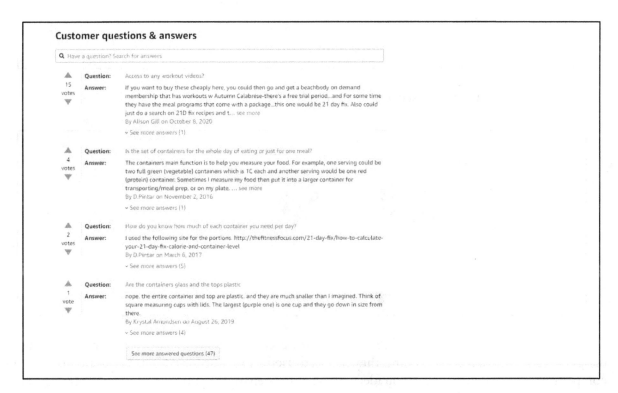

Another section feature customer reviews, and any images posted by customers.

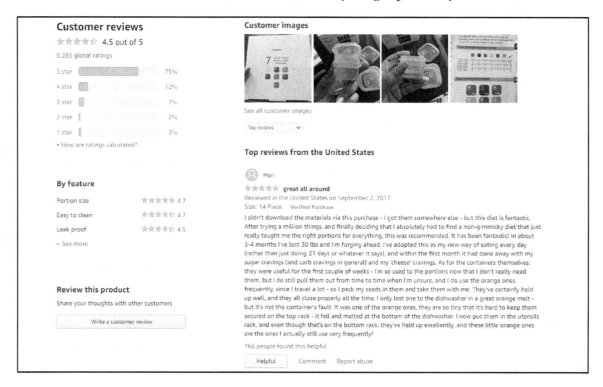

Finally, there is another section on products related to this item.

While these descriptions of the product featured and the listings of other products are all designed to help Amazon sell more, they are also useful to show you what has been working for competitors. Also, they will give you ideas on what to prepare for you own marketing strategy, such as creating ad copy with illustrations and producing promotional and informational videos with more details about your product.

Using Software to Help You Learn about Other Books

While you can search on Amazon directly, another tool to help you learn about your competitors in publishing is PublisherRocket, previously known as KDP Rocket. You can use it to find keywords, analyze your competition, do a search for competing books in your category, and additionally do a search by the keywords that Amazon uses. There are tutorials on how to use the system.

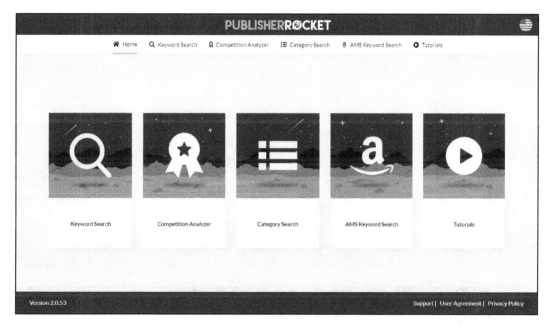

A good starting point is the keyword search. Say you're interested in books on fitness.. You can look for books on that subject by typing in "fitness."

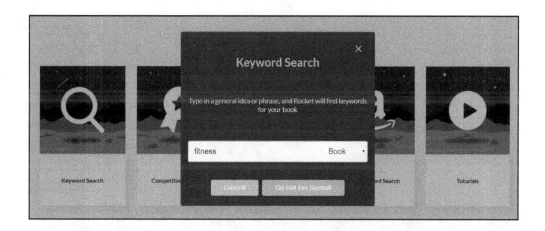

Your search will list a series of keywords, and you can analyze any one of these to show the number of competitors, their average monthly earnings, the number of searches for that keyword on Google and Amazon, and a competitive score, which indicates the competitiveness of a keyword.

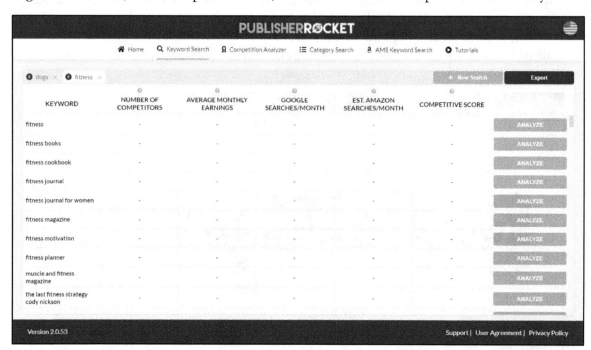

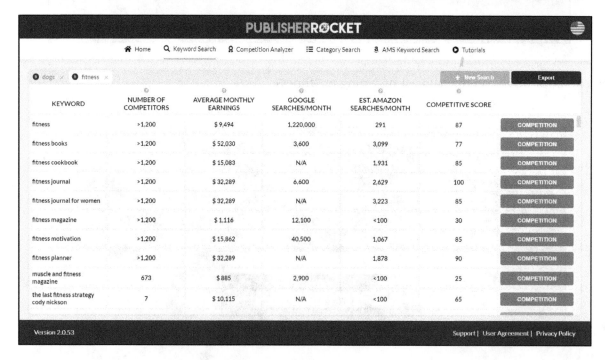

KEYWORD	NUMBER OF COMPETITORS	AVERAGE MONTHLY EARNINGS	GOOGLE SEARCHES/MONTH	EST. AMAZON SEARCHES/MONTH	COMPETITIVE SCORE	
fitness	>1,200	$ 9,494	1,220,000	291	87	COMPETITION
fitness books	>1,200	$ 52,030	3,600	3,099	77	COMPETITION
fitness cookbook	>1,200	$ 15,083	N/A	1,931	85	COMPETITION
fitness journal	>1,200	$ 32,289	6,600	2,629	100	COMPETITION
fitness journal for women	>1,200	$ 32,289	N/A	3,223	85	COMPETITION
fitness magazine	>1,200	$ 1,116	12,100	<100	30	COMPETITION
fitness motivation	>1,200	$ 15,862	40,500	1,067	85	COMPETITION
fitness planner	>1,200	$ 32,289	N/A	1,878	90	COMPETITION
muscle and fitness magazine	673	$ 885	2,900	<100	25	COMPETITION
the last fitness strategy cody nickson	7	$ 10,115	N/A	<100	65	COMPETITION

Next, using the Competition Analyzer, you can see the top 10 books on Amazon for that term, just like you might do the search directly on Amazon and do a search for books generally, which include paperbacks, hardcovers, Kindle, and audiobooks, or just look for Kindle books. But it is faster doing the search here.

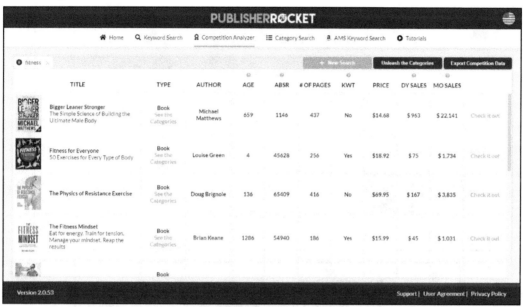

You can learn more about a particular book by clicking on that book. For instance, the first book *Bigger Leander Stronger* yields these results, which provides details about the book and what the author is doing to promote it. Plus it shows related books on the subject, which you can look at for more information on other competitors in the field. While Amazon is showing these books to invite readers to purchase them, this data provides a trove of competitor information you can use.

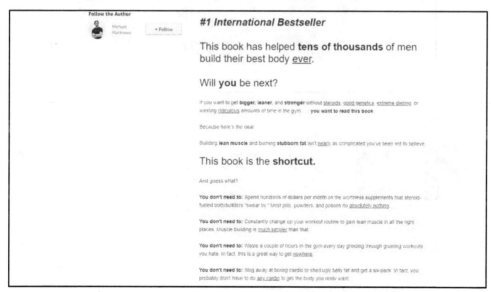

As you scroll down the first page, you'll see all kinds of information about this book and others on the same or a similar subject. Like many popular books, it will have a great many pages of reviews, a message from the publisher, and other books – in this case over 50 pages of information.

In this case, since the author has gotten extensive publicity, Amazon features that, along with editorial reviews from various publications.

WHO IS MIKE MATTHEWS?

I believe that everyone can achieve the body of his or her dreams, and my scientific approach to building muscle and losing fat has helped thousands of people build strong, lean, muscular, and healthy bodies.

My goal is to turn that number into hundreds of thousands and ultimately millions, so, if you're ready to build YOUR best body ever, then I'd love to help.

Thanks for your interest in my work, and I hope to hear from you soon!

AS FEATURED IN

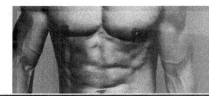

ARE YOU READY TO BUILD YOUR BEST BODY EVER? BUY THIS BOOK TODAY!

Editorial Reviews

Review

"If you want to use strength training for aesthetics, Mike is your source. Read this book, and read mine too, and come away with what you need to know. The rest will be up to you."
--Mark Rippetoe, author of *Starting Strength: Basic Barbell Training and Practical Programming for Strength Training*

"I highly, highly recommend *Bigger Leaner Stronger*. You don't just read it. You do it. And you see immediate changes and results."
--Hafthor "The Mountain" Björnsson, World's Strongest Man champion

"Nobody cuts through the fitness and nutrition confusion and clutter like Mike Matthews. And in *Bigger Leaner Stronger*, he draws on a powerful combination of time in the trenches and hard-core research to give you the straight talk about what actually works. This book is easy to read and incredibly effective. I highly recommend."
--Ben Greenfield, CEO of Kion & New York Times bestselling author of *Beyond Training: Mastering Endurance, Health & Life*

"*Bigger Leaner Stronger* is a super well-researched and practical guide to strength training that quickly cuts through the massive amount of BS and misinformation put out by the strength training, bodybuilding, weight gain and weight loss industries. I highly recommend adding this book to your library and referring to it frequently."
--Mark Divine, founder of SEALFIT and New York Times bestselling author of *The Way of the SEAL, Unbeatable Mind* and *8 Weeks to SEALFIT*

"Mike has written the encyclopedia of body recomposition for the twentieth century. A great book and a must-buy for beginners looking to get their feet wet."
--Martin Berkhan, fitness coach, pioneer, and author of *The Leangains Method*

"Mike Matthews stands alone in the fitness space. His books are based on scientific research and real-world results. *Bigger Leaner Stronger* changed my life. It can change yours too."
--Strauss Zelnick, "America's fittest CEO" and author of *Becoming Ageless: The Four Secrets to Looking and Feeling Younger Than Ever*

"In *Bigger Leaner Stronger*, Mike takes us back to the fundamentals of losing fat and building muscle--time-tested and science-backed strategies that have been obscured by a rising tide of popular hype and pseudoscience. The good news: it doesn't have to be that hard!"
--Alex Hutchinson, author of the New York Times bestseller *Endure: Mind, Body, and the Curiously Elastic Limits of Human Performance*

"Matthews has masterfully distilled many years of research into the essence of what makes guys bigger, leaner, and stronger. His training methods have worked better than anything else I've tried for improving my strength and physique. Get this book right now."
--Stephen Guise, international bestselling author of *Mini Habits*

"Mike Matthews has done it again. Great information backed by science, and complicated knowledge transformed into practical, applicable strategies. I loved *Bigger Leaner Stronger*. A must-read."
--Adam Schafer, co-host of top-ranked fitness and health podcast *Mind Pump*

Plus there is an extensive author interview, followed by product information on the book and videos for this and other books in the field.

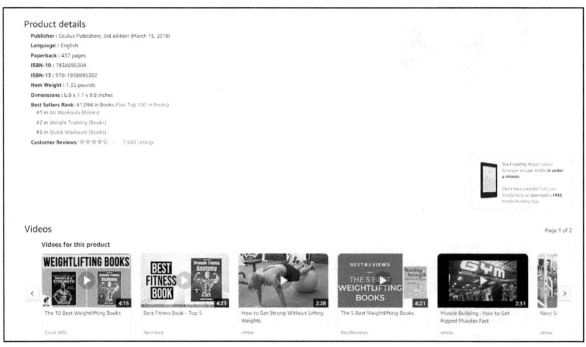

Then, comes more information on the author, related products, customer reviews, and other products that customers who viewed this book also viewed. Amazon truly collects a mine of information, and studying it to learn about what you competitors are doing will give you a wealth of knowledge to apply in your own marketing efforts.

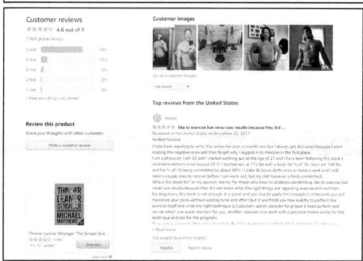

Additionally, you can do a search by the 12,000 categories in Amazon to see how many books are listed in the categories where your book might fit. Then, you can pick the categories and subcategories where you have the best chance of standing out. You can scroll down the list of main categories or list the category you are searching for, such "health and fitness."

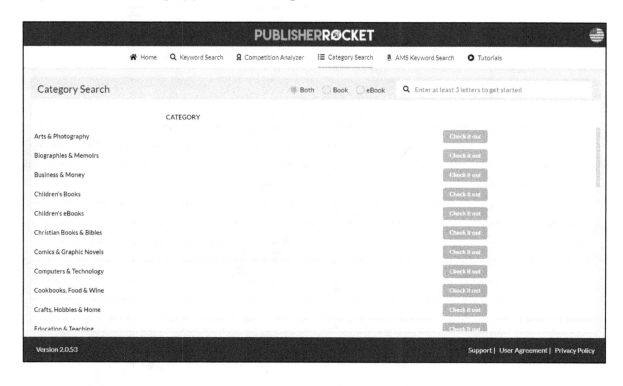

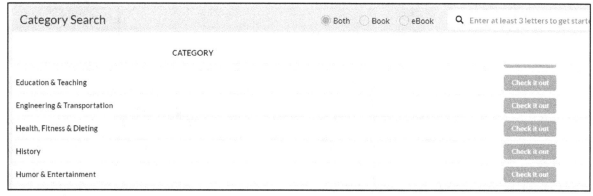

After you narrow down your search, you can see the number of books that have achieved Amazon Best Seller Rank (ASBR) for number #1 and top ten books in that category, and how many books you need to sell each day to achieve rank #1 or #10 in that category.

PUBLISHERROCKET

🏠 Home 🔍 Keyword Search 👤 Competition Analyzer ☰ Category Search 🅰 AMS Keyword Search ⏻ Tutorials

Both - Health, Fitness & Dieting   ← Back   🔍 Search Categories

CATEGORY	ABSR of #1	SALES to #1	ABSR of #10	SALES to #10	CATEGORY PAGE
Books > Health, Fitness & Dieting > Addiction & Recovery	579	100	3992	26	Check it out
Books > Health, Fitness & Dieting > Addiction & Recovery > Adult Children of Alcoholics	1720	74	25179	9	Check it out
Books > Health, Fitness & Dieting > Addiction & Recovery > Alcoholism	313	155	1266	60	Check it out
Books > Health, Fitness & Dieting > Addiction & Recovery > Drug Dependency	1059	69	5803	19	Check it out
Books > Health, Fitness & Dieting > Addiction & Recovery > Gambling	22668	9	64336	2	Check it out
Books > Health, Fitness & Dieting > Addiction & Recovery > Hoarding	15497	11	20313	10	Check it out
Books > Health, Fitness & Dieting > Addiction & Recovery > Obsessive Compulsive Disorder (OCD)	319	152	11824	12	Check it out
Books > Health, Fitness & Dieting > Addiction & Recovery > Smoking	5421	20	41914	5	Check it out
Books > Health, Fitness & Dieting > Addiction & Recovery > Substance Abuse	1244	61	5296	21	Check it out
Books > Health, Fitness & Dieting > Addiction & Recovery > Twelve-Step Programs	1407	54	11571	12	Check it out
Books > Health, Fitness & Dieting > Aging	359	136	1326	58	Check it out
Books > Health, Fitness & Dieting > Aging > Beauty, Grooming & Style	13636	11	81443	2	Check it out

Version 2.0.53   Support | User Agreement | Privacy Policy

PUBLISHERROCKET

🏠 Home 🔍 Keyword Search 👤 Competition Analyzer ☰ Category Search 🅰 AMS Keyword Search ⏻ Tutorials

Both - Health, Fitness & Dieting   ← Back   🔍 Search Categories

CATEGORY	ABSR of #1	SALES to #1	ABSR of #10	SALES to #10	CATEGORY PAGE
Kindle Store > Kindle eBooks > Health, Fitness & Dieting > Exercise & Fitness > Pregnancy	13848	14	261515	1	Check it out
Kindle Store > Kindle eBooks > Health, Fitness & Dieting > Exercise & Fitness > Quick Workouts	2433	81	62971	4	Check it out
Kindle Store > Kindle eBooks > Health, Fitness & Dieting > Exercise & Fitness > Walking	4900	36	105808	1	Check it out
Kindle Store > Kindle eBooks > Health, Fitness & Dieting > Exercise & Fitness > Weight Training	2296	84	28434	10	Check it out
Kindle Store > Kindle eBooks > Health, Fitness & Dieting > Exercise & Fitness > Yoga	3144	67	43981	7	Check it out
Kindle Store > Kindle eBooks > Health, Fitness & Dieting > Nutrition	1224	107	6916	22	Check it out
Kindle Store > Kindle eBooks > Health, Fitness & Dieting > Nutrition > Antioxidants & Phytochemicals	35237	9	124034	1	Check it out
Kindle Store > Kindle eBooks > Health, Fitness & Dieting > Nutrition > Food Allergies	12102	14	170409	1	Check it out
Kindle Store > Kindle eBooks > Health, Fitness & Dieting > Nutrition > Macrobiotics	1924	92	62360	4	Check it out
Kindle Store > Kindle eBooks > Health, Fitness & Dieting > Nutrition > Vitamins & Supplements	15211	14	58899	4	Check it out
Kindle Store > Kindle eBooks > Health, Fitness & Dieting > Personal Health	1	6390	2235	85	Check it out

Version 2.0.53   Support | User Agreement | Privacy Policy

Once you have narrowed down the categories to check out, you can see the top sellers in that category, such as in Exercise and Fitness, where top selling *Bigger Leaner Stronger* book is #9 in the "fitness" search in the combined fields of exercise and fitness.

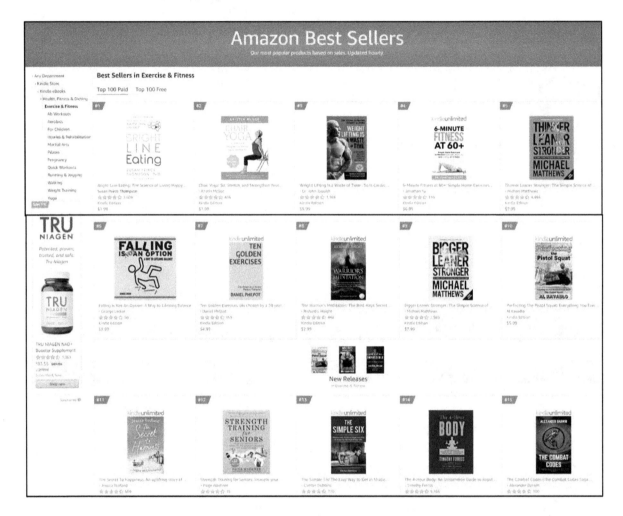

In short, you can use this PublisherRocket tool to get even more market intelligence about competing books in your field than you can get with an Amazon search alone. This detailed information can help you decide the best categories for listing your book where you will have the most visibility and the best chance of reaching number one or at least achieving top ten status. Plus you can learn from your competitors in looking at their cover designs, which can provide a guide for designing your own cover – or having a designer use these as a guide for you. You can also see what other kind of supporting materials they have for their books, such as editorial book reviews, reviews from readers, author interviews, reader reviews, videos, and other materials, which will give you ideas for what to include in promoting your own book on Amazon. You might use that material on your website or landing page for your book as well.

CHAPTER 2: FINDING COMPETITORS ON CLICKBANK

Besides selling on Amazon, a top market for sales for a wide variety of products is ClickBank, where you not only sell directly to customers but seek to create a network of affiliates. They market your product through their own websites, email lists, social media promotions, and advertising. Signing up affiliates is a way to get a whole sales team promoting your product, which can include everything from books, online courses, and software to physical products of all types.

You can set up your account once you are ready to sell your product, but first check out the competition in your field. This way you can see what is the most popular, along with the sales, marketing, and promotional material used to promote that product to the end customer and the sales affiliate.

To get started with your research, go to the site, where you'll see the four main opportunities – to shop, sell your own products, find products of other sellers to promote, and learn how to make money through online marketing.

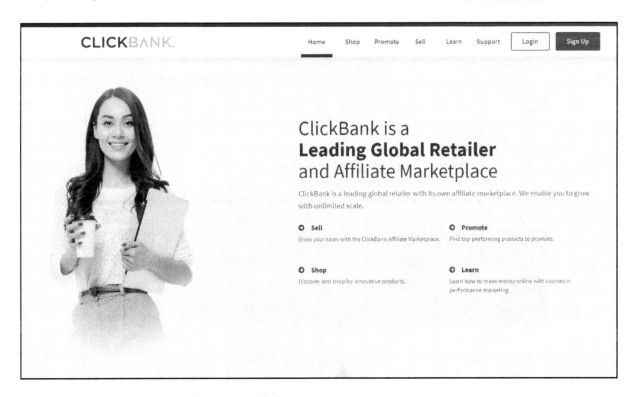

The introductory shop page shows the featured and other products in nine major product categories. If your product or product line fit into any of these categories, this can be a profitable place for sales. The categories are: Arts and Entertainment; E-Business and E-Marketing; Games; Health and Fitness; Homes and Gardens; Parenting and Families; Self-Help; and Spirituality, New Age, and Alternate Beliefs.

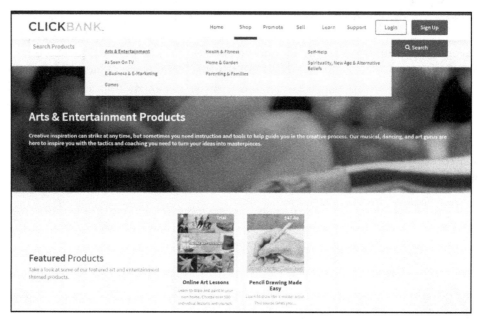

The sales page shows a few featured products, which are especially popular, such as some introductory how-to products. Should multiple products be selling well in a category, there will be an additional section for subcategories, such as in the E-Business and E-Marketing Category.

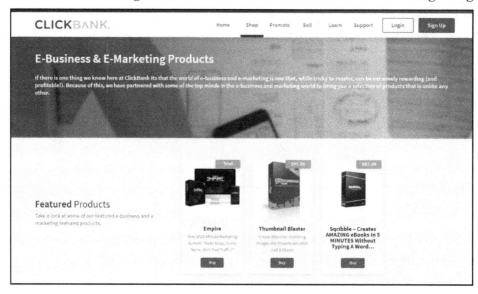

To illustrate, here are three E-Business and E-Marketing subcategories, where you can click on a subcategory to learn more. In this case, the featured products are each placed in one of the subcategories.

To take one more example, here's a listing of featured products in the Health and Fitness Category, with the products categorized by sub-category.

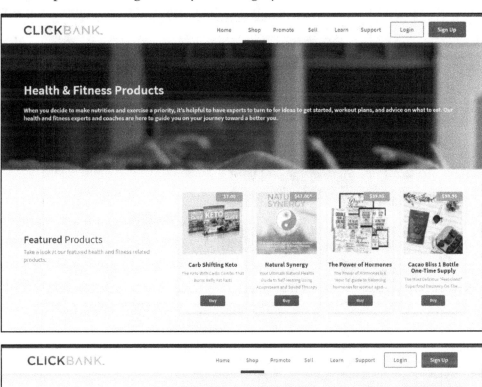

Should you want to sell your own products or promote others' products, ClickBank provides more information on how to do that, along with an invitation to set up an account.

You'll see examples of success stories from other sellers and learn about the advantages of selling on the ClickBank marketplace.

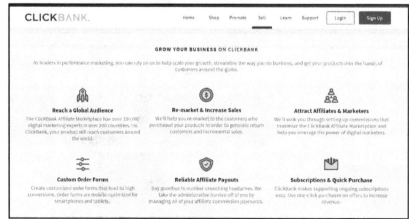

In order to do the background research on the competition, you have to join, either to sell your own products or become an affiliate, but there is no charge until you want to sell your own product and it is approved.

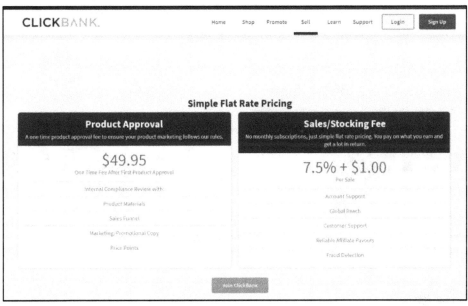

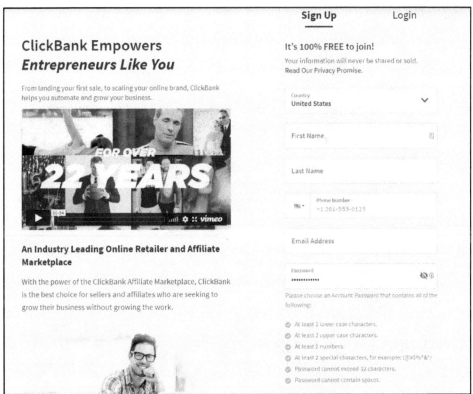

To become an affiliate and get commissions, you likewise need to set up an account. Even if you want to sell your own products, it can be helpful to become an affiliate, since you can learn about sales techniques which you can apply to your own product sales.

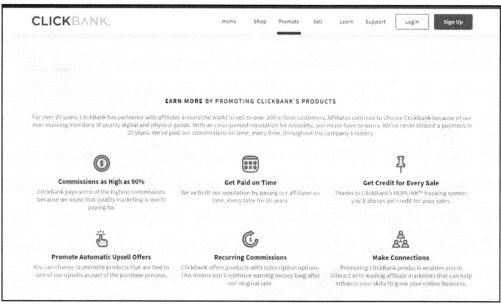

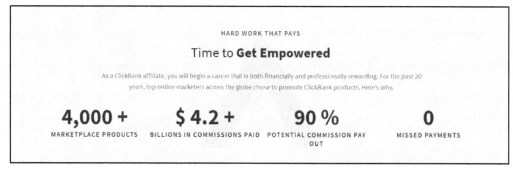

Finally, if you want to learn more about digital sales and marketing, ClickBank offers courses through Spark marketing – about 100 courses for $37 a month.

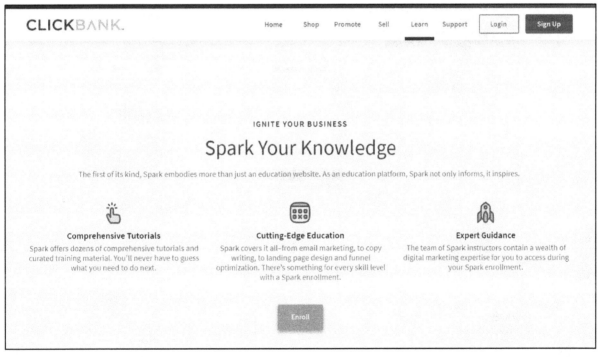

Some videos about the Spark program will give you more details.

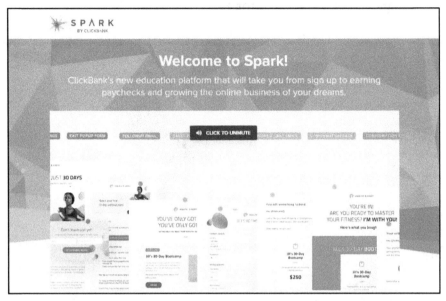

After you set up your account, you will see the products for sale in different categories and how well they are doing, along with the marketing materials, including videos, used to sell them. Then, you can use this information to knowledgeably make decisions about choosing, positioning, and promoting your own products – or in selecting other products from other sellers to promote.

Once you log in, go to the Marketplace to see the different categories. Then, visit the category or categories which interest you.

Besides the categories listed when you first visit the ClickBank site, there are nearly two dozen categories on a complete list:

I'll use the products in a few categories – Health and Fitness, Business, and Self-Help to illustrate, since these are very popular categories for different types of products – from physical products to online courses and books.

In assessing the products you might be competing with, consider the product's popularity and gravity, which is the number of affiliates marketing the product. The product's popularity is based on its ranking from #1 on in a category. The gravity is indicated by its number – the higher the number, the more affiliates are marketing the product. Together, these two measures indicate what people are interested in. Should a product do well on both measures, that not only shows the product is selling well but is attracting other sellers. Then, you can look more closely at these top performers in your market to both learn from your competitors in it and make your competing product different or better.

Promoting Health and Fitness Products

To illustrate, here's a listing of products in the Health and Fitness Category.

You'll notice that the products are listed by rank, indicating which products are selling the most, though they can be ordered by other criteria, including average conversion amount and gravity. The two factors to focus on are <u>rank</u> and <u>gravity.</u>

If you look more closely at the top three listings, you'll see that they have very salesy sales copy which emphasizes the benefits and value of the product. They each list a price showing the average price of an initial purchase, and if there is a recurring charge, that price is listed, followed by the gravity number. The sales description also provides an affiliate page with a marketing package which affiliates can use to promote the product. Various attributes of the product are listed by symbols, such as a U.S. flag for the English language, two arrows for a recurring billing or a $ sign for a single billing, a square for a physical package, an arrow pointing up indicating a reselling opportunity, and a phone to indicate that the product supports mobile traffic. Additionally, the listing will indicate if there is a subcategory, such as Dietary Supplements, which is listed under the product's Stats.

While these top products cost over $100 each, there are some products with lower pricing, such as for a book of remedies. So you can sell a product for much less; though be sure to price it to allow for an affiliate commission of 60-90%; a 60-70% commission is typical.

Next, do an analysis of the promotional materials and sales message that sells this top selling product to give you ideas of how to market your own product. For example, with Resurge, the first message is to watch a video about the product. When you do, you'll see the video also describes why people should want what the product offers and the simplicity of taking it in two minutes to overcome various health problems. The video also describes what led up to developing the product, the scientific research behind it, and the many people who experienced weight loss, more energy, and a more youthful appearance. Finally, the video ends by offering the special low price available now, and lists the prices for a 30, 60, or 90 day supply.

Though the video lasts for about 10 minutes, it is expertly done with a mix of stock footage and video of the developer of the product. Here are some screen shots of clips from the video, followed by the product offer, which urges viewers to buy now. Then, I've included examples of sales and promotional materials for the next two top products, since it is a good idea to check out the approach of at least three of your top competitors, so you can see a pattern of what works for the top products in your category.

The Resurge video emphasizes that there is a formula of nutrients which you take for two minutes before going to bed in order to experience the deep sleep that promotes a better metabolism and regenerates your body. The video begins by showing the product developer's struggles which led him to discovering the formula that worked to achieve that deep sleep, intermixed with images of people facing a variety of health problems. Then, the video shows others finding great improvement after taking the pills formula. It also mixes in offer for a special price if you buy now.

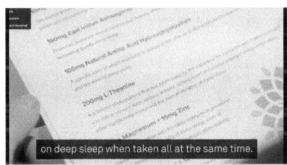

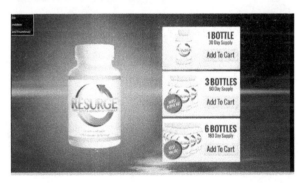

Then, the video concludes with directions to look at the offer below, followed by three ways to offer and more information about the product.

Here are some more examples. Most start off with a short promotional video explaining why this is such a great product and why it is now available with a special offer, though some still use just compelling introductory copy.

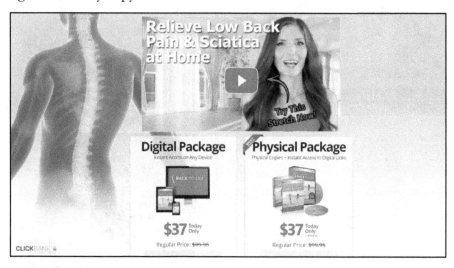

This one begins with just copy, yet it is number two in the field, so you don't necessarily need a video if you have a compelling message and a strong product. The copy describes why you need this tonic, shows the product, and explains the offer, which features a super low price if you act now and get the product while supplies last.

Now apply this approach to looking at product listings from competitors in your field to see the way they present their product and offer. Ideally, as most offers do, you might start off with a compelling video about your product, which includes a story and examples that show the need for it, a description of its benefits, a close-up of the product, and the price of various offers. End your pitch with a final message of why the viewer should buy it now.

To illustrate how the search for the top products and how they are presented and sold in other industries, I'll give two more examples – from the business and self-help industries, which are very popular in this marketplace.

Promoting Business and E-Business Products

Here are some business and e-business examples. There are a number of subcategories, and these illustrations are from the Marketing and Sales subcategory. Before you decide to sell your own products in that category, look at both the ranking and the gravity figure, which indicates the number of affiliates. If the gravity is very low, it might still be instructive to see the marketing and sales approach of your competitors, but this may not be the best category to enter with your own products because of the small number of affiliates marketing these products.

On the other hand, if you have an e-business, that will do much better. For example, the top three products have gravity ratings ranging from 170 to 214, showing that these have many affiliates selling the program. And some of them may promote the product on various platforms, such as through the social media. For example, I have seen many Facebook ads for Speechelo, which is the top selling text-to-speech program.

Here's how Speechelo promotes its product – no video, but compelling images and sales copy which first presents what Speechelo does, the advantages of the program, some testimonials, and how you can get it now for a low reduced price.

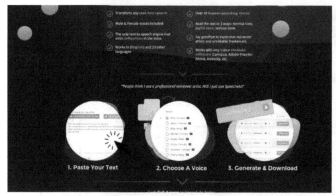

As Speechelo's approach shows, you don't need a video to sell your product. But check out at least three competitors' products in your chosen marketing category to see what approach they are using. For example, here is another sales pitch in this E-Business – E-Marketing Category. This one begins with a short video that invites you to put in your email to get more information on a secret algorithm that can make you a lot of money. It's an approach used to get an email, so the seller can send you more information, rather than inviting you to buy now.

If you don't respond right away without seeing the video, you will get a message to put in your name and email to get your spot. If you respond, a 5-minute video with mostly stock images will explain how much you can earn with this secret algorithm, so reserve your spot now.

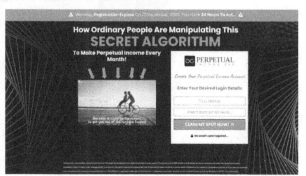

This next sales pitch uses videos along with an upsell, so you gain access to the basic program, but then there are one or more opportunities to add on additional features to gain even more benefits. There may even be a coupon to reduce the price so you buy now. For example, you can get additional templates, images, or content; training on using the product; software to help you find more clients or work; and other benefits. The following product called Sqribble for creating e-books uses this approach. The initial buy-in is for only $35, and a couple further reduces the price to only $20, but when you make a purchase, you have an option to add in training for another $9. Then, after you pay, before your offer is finalized, you get a series of upsells, and if you turn one down, you still get the next upsell. It's an ideal approach when you have several related products that appeal to the same audience.

Here's the beginning of the Sqribble series to illustrate. The pitch starts with a short headline announcing what the service is. Then, it features a video, which you just have to click to play. In this case, the video uses animation and cartoon characters to share the message, whereas other videos which focus on personal benefits, such as health and financial success, generally feature images and video clips of individuals in the target audience.

Here's how the video uses a cartoon robot and a man working at a computer, along with a text message explaining how well the Sqribble program can save you work.

Then, a video of a cartoon character watching a computer screen shows the various things the software program can do. The video ends up with some close-ups of the product and an invitation to order now.

The sales copy under the video shows off the product, lists some benefits, and shows some examples of books created from the templates offered by the software.

The sales copy also includes another video demonstrating how easy it is to use the software – which is a good use of a video if you have a product where you can show someone using it. Then, after more sales copy extolling the benefits for the product, there is an offer to get it now. If you still need convincing, testimonials from over a dozen customers express their satisfaction with the product.

After that, there is a recap of all of the benefits, followed by another offer to buy now, another listing of benefits in a different format, and an introduction to the creators of the program to help personalize the product.

If there's an upsell, the pitch usually begins after you complete your first product purchase. Whether you purchase the upsell or not, if there are additional upsells, you will get the next upsell and then the next, although sometimes an upsell will depend on you previously purchasing the previous sale in the series, such as if you offer the basic purchase for an introductory price such as $25-50; a professional or premium upsell for $75-100; and the elite upsell for $125-150.

In any case, the first upsell will typically provide additional ways to use the product or more content you can apply with this method, such as in the Sqribble upsell I received after I bought the initial order with training and applied the coupon. The upsell offered more templates, additional articles, and more images for $87 more.

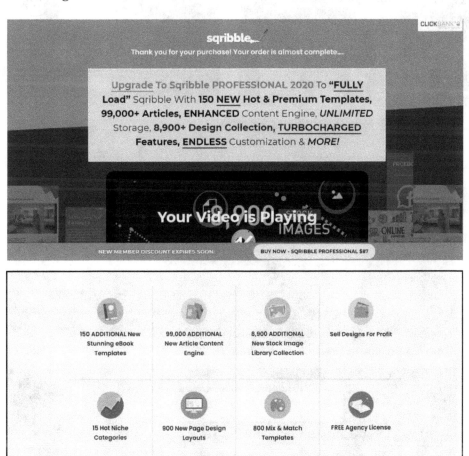

Then, just as extensive sales copy pitched the original purchase, more sales copy promoted the features and benefits of the professional upgrade. One big appeal was to price by contrasting the high value of each element of the product offered with the much lower price of purchasing it. To that end, the sales copy itemized the value of the templates, additional images, and other components which was vastly higher than the price of the product. Then, the video ended with a recap of the benefits of the upgrade, an offer, and a 30-day satisfaction guarantee.

The third upsell in the series offered a subscription to build on my original or upgraded purchase. This is another type of upsell used to gain customer loyalty through a membership in a program which has a recurring monthly or annual fee. In this case, the pitch was for getting additional e-book templates to create e-books for myself or for customers with even more variety. And again, the pitch ended with a "buy it now" offer to get it for a one-time low price – in this case $44 – instead of $149 a month.

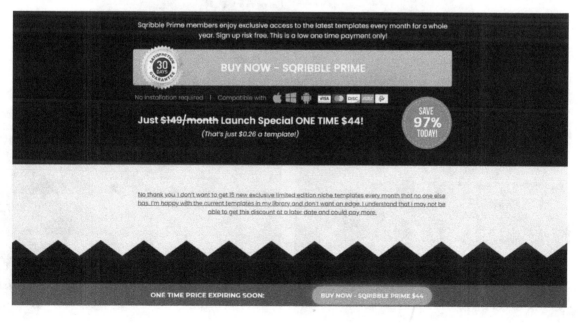

Then, whether I bought the second or third upsell, another upsell offered an opportunity to further enhance the original purchase by creating book covers with interactive and animated images. Doing so would make the e-book even more impressive and generate more and higher sales. And again the pitch ended with an offer of big savings for getting it now - $74 instead of $247, with a 30 day right of return.

Finally, should a customer want to use this product to get more work creating e-books for customers, a final pitch offered automated software to help one get more jobs creating these books. In this case, this "find more clients" software was offered as an upsell for this product, though the appeal of this software might make it a stand-alone product.

In turn, this connection with another product is a way to expand your sales by finding other products to sell that might fit with your product offerings or finding other sellers or affiliates to sell your product.

For example, this fifth upsell indicates how much an individual can make writing e-books and finding jobs from a variety of freelance job services by using the AutoJobFinder software.

After explaining how the software automates the process of applying for jobs, the sales copy invites purchasers to buy this additional product now.

Finally, after a listing of the many benefits of earning more money with this software, the video features another picture of the software followed by an offer of a very low one-time payment, compared to the high cost of purchasing it after the offer expires at any time. Then the cost will be much higher -- $2023 -- for purchasing it each year for five years compared to paying only a $99 one-time payment now.

In short, this upsell method can be extremely powerful if you have a product or program that lends itself to upsells. These can be not only extensions of your own product or you can incorporate related products from others. To recap, you start with a low price for the first upsell, and progressively increase the price on further upsells that offer more and more value. And sometimes sellers use downsells if a prospective buyer doesn't buy a higher priced item, but might find a lower priced item appealing.

While these sales examples have featured products on ClickBank, this kind of promotion can be launched anywhere – such as on your website or using a link on the social media which goes to a landing page to sell the product.

Promoting Self-Help Products

For one more example, I'll illustrate the types of sales pitches in the self-help category, which has about a dozen subcategories. If you are not sure where your product fits or it could fit in multiple categories, a good way to decide on the category is to look at the gravity level for the top three or four listings in any relevant subcategory and compare them to see which have the highest gravity, and therefore the most appeal to affiliates to sell your product.

Say your product deals with improving self-esteem for success that might be especially appealing to public speakers. The listing might also fit in the motivational/transformational category. You might look at the other products in each of these categories where your product might fit and check the relevance of these products to yours. Then, if there is a good fit, consider the gravity level of these products to see which products are gaining the most interest from affiliates.

For example, the results in the whole Self-Help category and a General listing shows a lack of relevance for a product improving self-esteem. The top three products in the overall listing feature a Trump 2020 Gold Plated coin, a Lost Ways painkilling remedy, and a club called the Patriot Wholesale Club selling food without brand. Names with a gravity level of 57 to 90. Though the gravity level is relatively high, the products don't seem related to your product. In the General category, the product from the Awakened Millionaire Academy is focused financial freedom and a spiritual awakening, the Dreanneagram product features a new spin on Enneagrams, and the Black Belt Memory Course is focused on improving memory. While these products seem more relevant, the gravity ratings are very low – only 2 to 3 points. Thus, if you are deciding how to list your product, these categories fail the relevance or gravity test or both.

By contrast, when you look at specific categories, there's a better fit – and a more specific listing is better, because individuals looking for a product to help them will generally seek out a particular type of product. For example, a comparison of four relevant subcategories: Self-Esteem, Success, Motivational/Transformational, and Public Speaking looks like this.

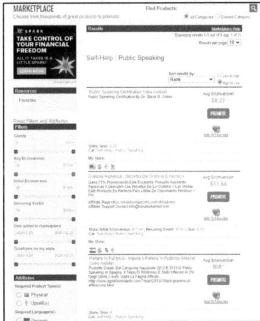

In doing a comparison, consider pricing, too, which will give you a ballpark or range for pricing your own product.

As you compare the listings in these subcategories, you'll notice that the products in the Self-Esteem category are focused on dating and feeling anxiety with others, so those products are less relevant to a self-help in business approach. Moreover, the gravity rating is very low – only 1.25-1.50. Then, when you look at the Public Speaking category, not only is the gravity rating low – 0 to .72, but two of the listings are for foreign languages products – in Spanish and Italian.

Alternatively, there's a much better fit with Success and Motivational/Transformational categories. In the Success category, the emphasis is on mental fitness and mastery with a much higher gravity rating of 12-30, while in the Motivational/Transformational category, the focus is on different systems for self-improvement, especially on manifesting what you want, including wealth, with a gravity rating of 10-20. So based on this, either category might be fitting, and you might consider drilling down into the top three sales approaches in each one. I'll describe assessing the sales approach briefly, since I've gone into detail on creating the sales copy for the Health and Fitness and Business categories. Since the Success category has a little higher gravity rating, I'll use that. Note that these products are all in English, have one-time purchase arrangements, are priced between $13-55, and have upsells, so you might consider setting up your product pricing and sales approach accordingly.

Once you do determine which category is the best fit for your product, consider the sales and promotional materials used to market these products as a guide for creating your own materials. For example, the sales pitch for these products include having a video, images of the company founder and spokesperson, extensive sales copy promoting the benefits and features, and the offer with the price, followed by upsells for those who buy the introductory product. This long copy approach echoes that in the pre-video era, when sales letters often went on for 15-25 pages, with copy broken up by repeated offers to buy now.

To illustrate, here's the first product in the Success category – on Dream Life Mastery, which touts its potential for earning a 90% commission on its hypnosis programs and 50% on its Dream Life Mastery system.

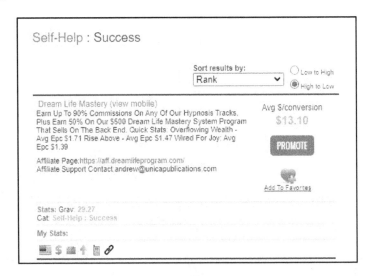

In this case, the program leader, Dr. Stephen G. Jones, uses a more traditional text-based model which emphasizes the program leader's expertise, followed by an introduction to the program and a link to attend a webinar or introductory class to learn more. But there's no buy now offer. That'll come for those who sign-up and view the online class. The opening page simply features the founder's picture, brief describes the advantages of the Dream Mastery program, and indicates the four ways it can help, along with a button to push for details.

Once you "Click here for details," the pitch is focused on getting you to attend the web-based class to learn more. It features a series of buttons to click to reserve your spot as you read through the copy about the program. You will then get a form to fill out to sign up and select a date – in this case instantly or at two times that day.

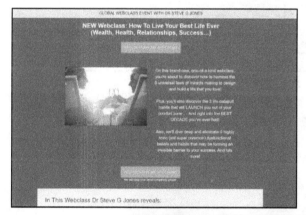

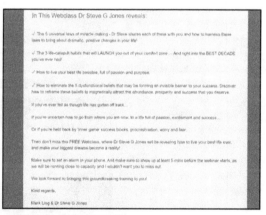

The second-highest ranking Ho'oponopono Mastery System uses a brief video from the founder and a course instructor, along with a traditional text-based promotion. The system features a certification program for a self-improvement system originating in Hawaii, which builds on ancient Hawaiian healing practices enabling one to heal oneself and others. They do so by getting rid of memories and data stored in the mind in order to allow light into the conscious and subconscious mind. The opening page of the sales pitch begins with a brief video to introduce a program, developer Dr. Joe Vitale, followed by photos of the three class teachers and a description of what you can gain through the program.

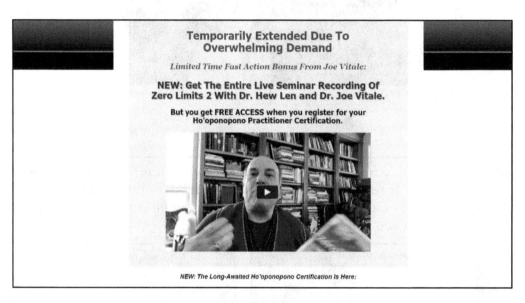

Master Authentic
Ho'oponopono And Unlock The
Ultimate Life Of Zero Limits

The Most In-Depth, Complete, And Definitive Online Training Ever Created
On Ho'oponopono, Including Material Never Released Until Now

Dr. Joe Vitale and Mathew Dixon Featuring Dr. Hew Len

- Get to the Euphoric and Connected State of "Zero"
- Open Yourself and Others to UNLIMITED Possibility
- Clean Your Perceptions to Create a New Reality
- Design Life Without Fear, Stress, or Boundaries
- Discover How Much Subconscious Memory Holds You Back
- Develop a Connection with the Divine Power
- All While Learning to Help and Teach Others

Discover the cleaning and healing power of
Ho'oponopono as a certified practitioner of
the modern form of an age-old practice.

Then, more details describe how to access the program on the Internet and the huge reduction in savings for buying now– only $39 instead of $397. The sales pitch concludes with an introduction to the instructors, for anyone who hasn't heard of the Ho'oponopono system, there is an explanation of what it is.

As a graduate of this certification program, you'll have the knowledge and skills required to effectively practice Ho'oponopono in your private practice, at home, with family, and anyone who seeks your help.

This course gives professional providers, specialists, and therapeutic providers an opportunity to embrace a modern version of an ancient self-cleaning art capable of eliminating self-imposed boundaries and connecting you to the divine.

Location: Internet

Dates: You may start any time.

Pace: Shortest Completion time is One Week. *3 Weeks of Study Recommended Before Certification Testing.*

Cost: $39 (Normally $397)

Registration Deadline: None. Register Anytime.

Cancellation Policy: Full refund available within 60 Days.

Minimum Age Requirement: 18.

Instructors:

Dr. Joe Vitale, Star Of The Hot Movie "The Secret" Author Of Over 50 Books Including The Attractor Factor And The Key

Mathew Dixon, World-renowned healing musician, producer of over 12-different healing projects with Dr. Joe Vitale, author and owner of Zero Limits Music.

Dr. Ihaleakala Hew Len, modern Ho'oponopono developer, therapist, and revolutionary spiritual, emotional, and material problem solving expert.

Provided Instructional Text: *Ho'oponopono Practitioner Certification Guidebook* provides 8 chapters of background information, history of Ho'oponopono, modern adaptations, details, and instructions for course completion and certification.

Video Seminar Instruction: 8 video lessons and a total of 6 hours and 40 minutes of seminar-style instruction introduce you to never-before-seen footage of Dr. Joe Vitale's *ZERO LIMITS* event featuring Dr. Hew Len and 4+ additional contributors. Following their video instruction, you'll learn the fundamentals of Ho'oponopono for private and professional practice.

Certification Exam: Exam details are provided at the end of the course. Cost is included.

Upon completion of your training, you will be certified by the Global Sciences Foundation to practice Modern Ho'oponopono.

About Ho'oponopono

Modern Ho'oponopono is an adaptation of an ancient Hawaiian problem-solving technique that allows practitioners and subjects working with therapeutic or wellness providers to emotionally and mentally let go of conscious and subconscious memory.

Through a "ZERO LIMITS" cleaning process, developed by Dr. Ihaleakala Hew Len, practitioners are able to move past perceived reality and to the point of zero.

During this process, practitioners are able to connect to experience a euphoric awakening, connecting to the divine to receive inspiration while clearing away limiting beliefs.

Ho'oponopono uses a 4-phrase mantra combined with a mindset shift you'll learn in this certification course to clean the data of our memories and help us retake 100% responsibility for everything in life, good, bad, and indifferent.

Then, after explaining the value of the program, the sales copy features images of the guidebook and the DVD discs with course content, though the actual course is set up online for viewing and downloading. The pitch concludes with a sample of the certification one receives for completing the training, an offer to enroll now with a 60-day cancellation policy, answers to additional questions about the course, and contact information.

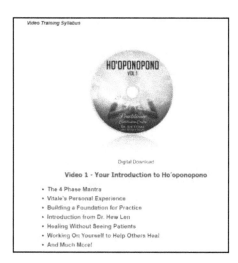

Finally, in this last example of a sales pitch, you can watch a video or see the sales copy text. The video begins with images of successful people in different fields, followed by images of a mountain climber ascending to the top, with the message that you can live your dreams.

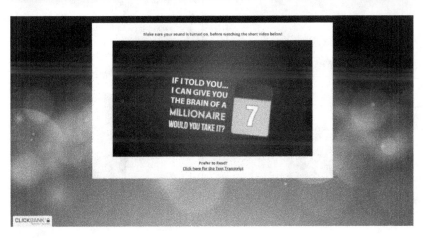

If you view the text for the video, you see a traditional sales message with benefits, features, testimonials, the offer, more sales copy, the offer again, still more sales copy, and the offer and copy repeated several more times, along with a money back guarantee. The text has the same message as in the video, but you can see the whole sales pitch more quickly, though many may find the video more powerful and modern to many.

Here are some highlights from the text message. As in the video, it starts off by suggesting that if you use the richest and happiest people in the world as a model, you too can similarly achieve your dreams and gain wealth. The copy includes examples of how the developer of the program overcame difficulties to achieve great success and concluded that the secret to this success is acquiring a millionaire's way of thinking – the "millionaire's brain".

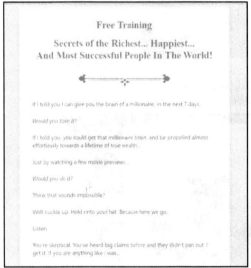

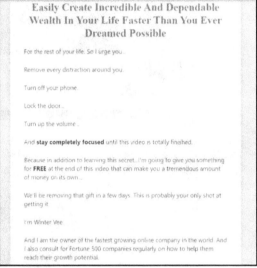

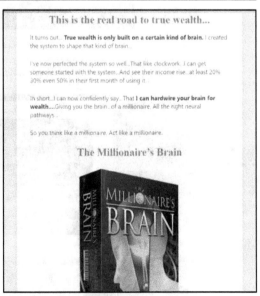

Then, after some testimonials and more sales copy about the value of the product, the focus turns to the product – the Millionaire Mindset.

The copy concludes with a series of pitches for the product followed by more praise for the product's benefits and why you should get it now. Again and again, the image of the product and copy about it is repeated, along with a buy button so you can make a purchase at any time. Plus, as with most offers, there is a money back guarantee if you're not satisfied.

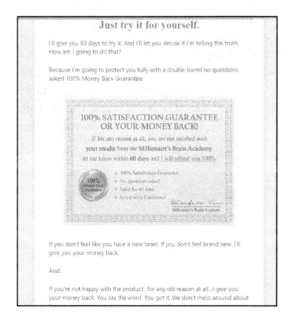

Using a Competition Assessment for Any Product

Now that you have gained an understanding of how to assess the sales and marketing approach of your competitors in different fields, you can apply this assessment to any type of product, whether it's an online or physical product or a service packaged as a product, such as a series of seminars, workshops, and classes.

This assessment approach can also work in creating your sales campaign on any platform and in creating ad copy for your website or for a landing page linked to a social media campaign. While ClickBank is a great nonexclusive market best suited for certain types of products, you can apply this kind of analysis of your competitors and their sales approach in any market.

To recap, first think about where you might best categorize your product based on several factors, which include the relevance of the products in that category to your product and their success in attracting sales and affiliate sellers. In ClickBank, this is measured by the product's ranking and gravity; on Amazon, this is measured by the rank in a category, which is based on the level of sales of products in that category.

Once you have identified your top competitors, look at their advertising approach for ideas. This analysis will show what kind of ad pitch they are using, such as video, videos and text, or images with sales copy – and the range of pricing in your field.

This sales copy is very important, so unless you are a good writer of marketing and promotional materials, it is best to hire an experienced ad copy writer. Ask for referrals in your business network or search online for these writers. Be sure to ask for credentials and examples of work they have done to help you decide who to hire, based on the type of campaign you want – video, video and text, or text only.

Additionally, consider the possibility of using your competitors' websites to promote your own products, or perhaps you might engage in joint promotions and advertising with your competitors. For example, when you visit your competitor's websites or the websites where they advertise, it may be possible to advertise your products there too. Or if you have related but not directly competitive products, possibly you might do joint mailings to your email lists or joint ads on the social media. You might also jointly reach out to be speakers or panelists in your field.

If your competitors have an email listed, send them a letter explaining who you are and what you want to do. Or if they ask for an initial contact through a contact form on your website or landing page, fill that out. Include your contact information and reasons for contacting them.

CHAPTER 3: CHECKING THE COMPETITOR WEBSITES

Another way to learn from your competitors is to look at their websites. You can use that information to improve your own website, as well as get insights about their advertising, links to other websites, and more. Two tools to help you do this are BuiltWith.com and SimilarWeb.com, which are online services with free and paid upgraded accounts. BuiltWith provides a look at the behind-the-scenes website technology, while SimlarWeb provides user and visitor information. I'll describe BuiltWith in this chapter and SimilarWeb in the next.

A Nuts and Bolts Look at their Website

The BuiltWith service can give you all sorts of information about the web technologies used by your competitors' websites, such as whether they use shopping carts or analytics, their hosting service, and the amount of traffic they get. You can also learn about their market share in different countries. Besides better understanding what your major competitors are doing, you can incorporate selected technologies in your own website.

Unless you are skilled at designing websites, discuss these options with your web designer. He or she can advise you on what changes or additions you might make for your site.

The BuiltWith home page illustrates the different information you can obtain.

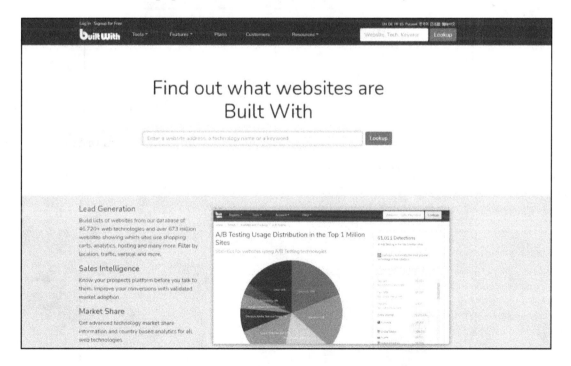

The site also provides information on the technologies your competitors or you use.

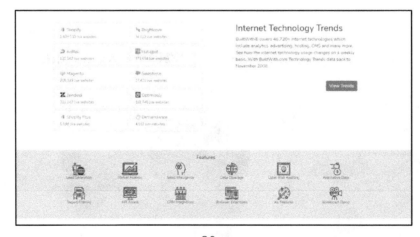

To learn about a competitor's website – possibly one you have learned about from your research on Amazon or ClickBank, enter its name in the search field. To illustrate, I'll use one of my websites – MyPromeo.com – which features a video creation service

Here's a Technology Profile, which indicates the various widgets, web servers, email services, and other technologies used in building my website. You may find components listed which you never heard of before, as I did, but you can discuss them with your website designer. While I using this service for my first free trial lookup, there's an option to get unlimited lookups from an upgrade offer -- $99 a year.

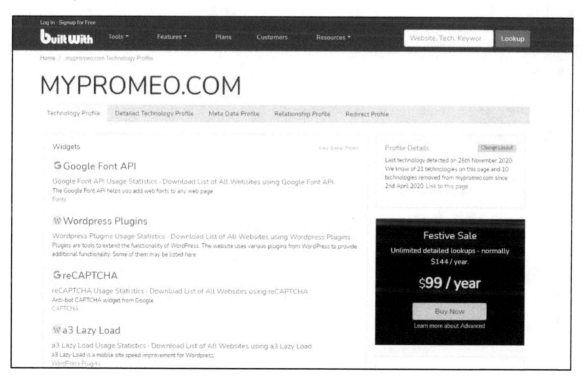

Here are even more technology components of the website.

Digging Even Deeper

To drill down further, you can look at the Detailed Technology Profile. Of special interest are the listings for E-Commerce, Audio/Visual Media, Web Hosting Providers, and Web Servers.

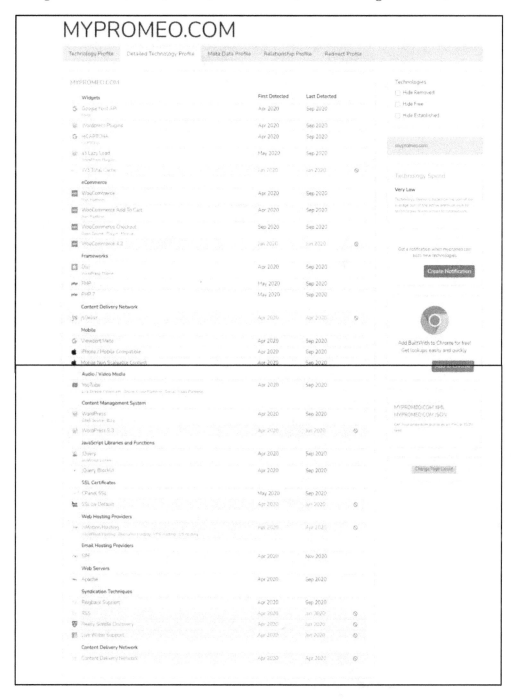

The Relationship Profile indicates the connections or links the site has with other websites. In this case, the links are to my own websites, though most competitors will have many more sites, especially if they have many affiliate relationships. You can use the listed sites to visit and perhaps contact them about being an affiliate for your products. Then, too, their site might be a good place to advertise your products and services.

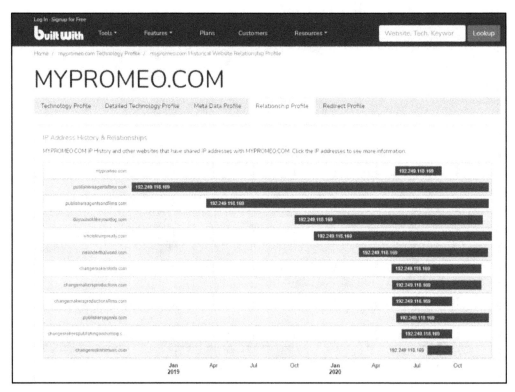

It may also be possible to get Metadata or a Redirect profile. But if the site has blockers against bots, that may prevent you from getting metadata, as occurred on my website. If there is no redirection from another site, there will be no data for this either.

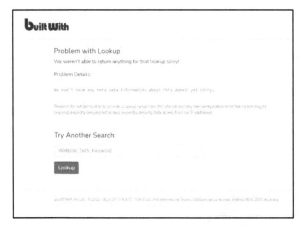

Additionally, you can learn about the Frameworks and Advertising components that provide usage statistics about websites using different types of themes and advertising.

You can obtain reports on the customers of various commerce sites, such as Shopify. With a paid account, you can drill down to get customers that match selected keywords, locations, or other information, giving you a better idea of your competitor's target market, which you could market to, as well.

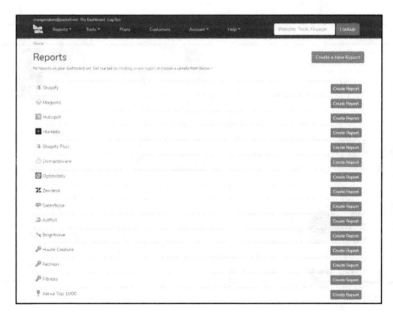

You can also create different types of reports about your competitors, and you can create lists based on the keywords used on your competitors' websites.

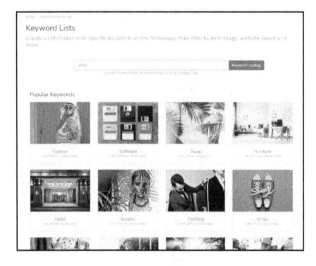

For example, when looking for competitors for the MyPromeo video site, I looked for sites with video in their name. You can further limit the number of sites listed with further targeting, such as for location, use of certain markets such as Shopify, sales, and the level of traffic. Then, you can select the way to filter your report.

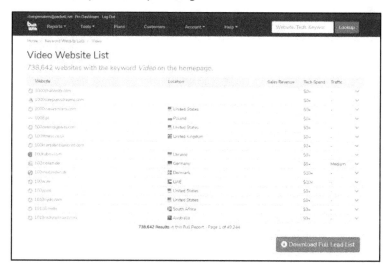

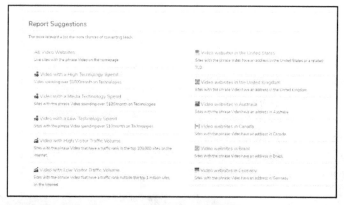

You can see suggestions for other types of targeting, such as by clicking the Ideas tab.

If you want to see or download a more complete listing in a report, there are various pricing plans. These are fairly pricy – from $229 to $995 a month or $225 to $9950 a year. But you can get some initial insights with the free plan, until you find this kind of website analysis sufficiently useful to sign up for a monthly or yearly fee. Or perhaps you might sign up and use the program for a month, and do all of your competitor research then.

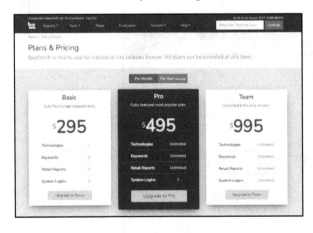

Here are some examples of the different types of filtering that is possible, such as by Technology Market Share and Technology Spend, though you will get a reminder to create a paid account if you want to see a complete list.

In the case of website verticals, those are the websites in your field which are listed in the Business and Industry or Technology and Computing category. In my case, I'm looking at video websites in the U.S., and I'm only seeing three of five listings this category with a free account.

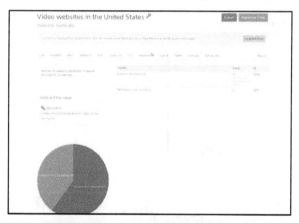

You can also use BuiltWith to get Report Ideas and find websites using certain marketing sites, such as Shopify.

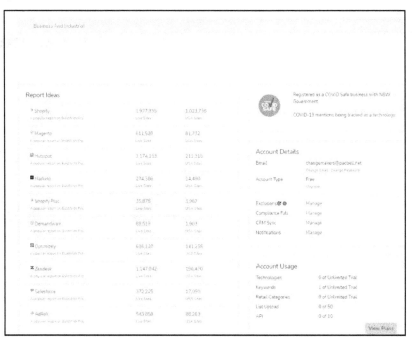

You can do a search for sites based on your keyword, such as "video," and then add more filters, such as Filter by Category to target your search.

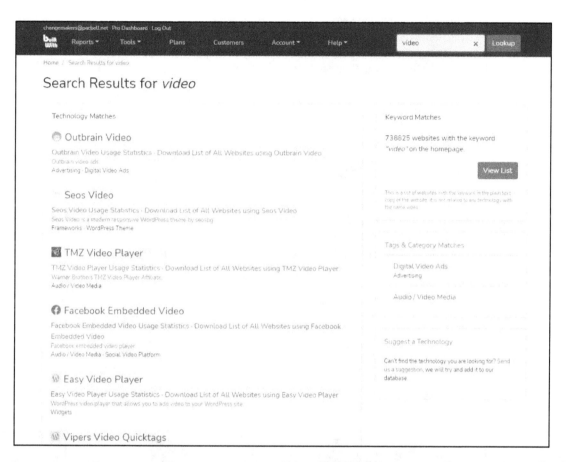

As you find new competitor websites, you can create a report based on that.

However, with a free account, any reports are limited to results based on only 50 websites.

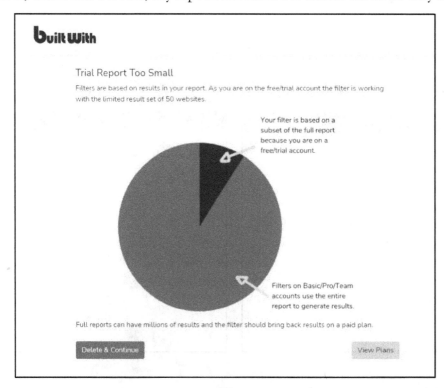

If you want more information on how to better find information on your competitors, you can find answers on doing research on creating reports from the site's extensive Knowledge Base, and from other tools the site provides for obtaining and organizing information.

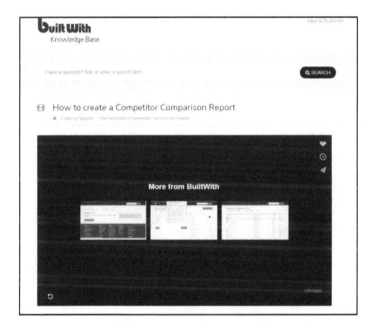 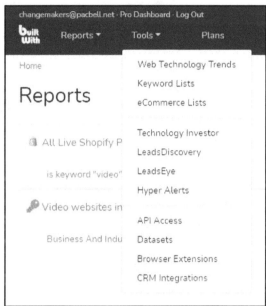

For more information on who uses this site and who's behind it, here's a listing of the company's major users and some testimonials. It already has 750,000 users, who have used it to learn about the websites of interest to them.

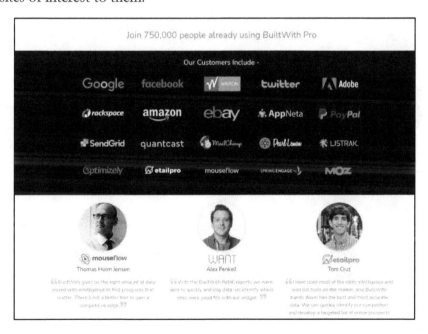

Once you learn about your competitors' websites and who links to them or advertises on their site, you can visit these websites and ask about advertising on their site with a similar product or possible engaging in joint promotions. To find these other websites, look at the relationships profile for a website or see who has ads there. You can then enter the domain name for the websites or click on the ads to go to the website or landing page to find out how to contact them.

CHAPTER 4: GAINING EVEN MORE INFORMATION ON YOUR COMPETITORS

Learning about Your Competitors with SimilarWeb

Another site where you can learn even more about your competitors is SimilarWeb. It's also a fairly pricy service at $199 a month or $167 monthly if you sign up for a year. But you can try it out for one day for free to learn what you can. Then, if you find it is useful, you can try it for a month or two to learn what you can.

The site is especially helpful for learning the major sources of traffic to your competitors' websites, which can suggest markets for you. You can additionally learn where they are advertising, what ads are receiving the most clicks, the different keywords on their site, and which ones are pulling in the most traffic. Then, you can increase your own traffic by using the keywords and advertising approach they use. Plus you can learn if they have affiliates, which ones are driving more traffic their way, and what keywords and advertising they are using.

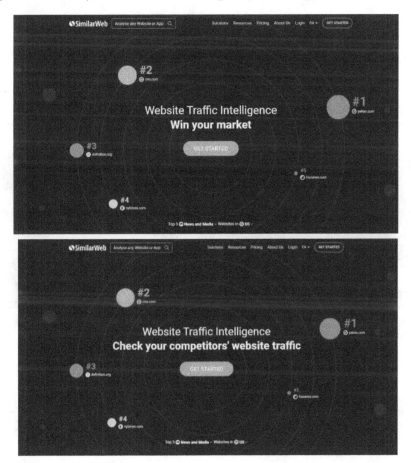

In effect, you are going behind the scenes to obtain digital marketing intelligence to learn the marketing strategies your competitors are using in different markets. As the site's home page proclaims, the goal is to "Win your market," and a key strategy for doing so is to "Check your competitors' website traffic."

Then, by learning the sources of your competitor's traffic and the marketing strategies that work best for them, you can adopt them increase your own traffic and market share and thereby increase your – ROI -- the return on the money you spend on marketing.

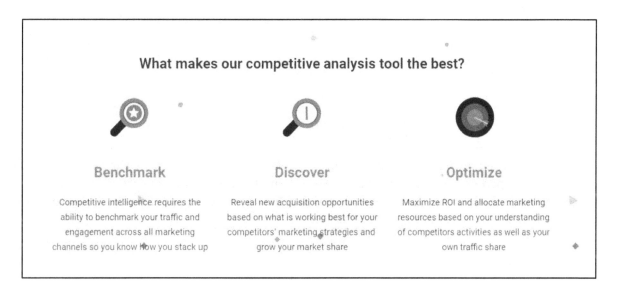

For example, you can look at which approaches are working better for companies using different channels, such as email marketing, social media, referrals from affiliates, organic search, and paid search. Then, you can adjust what you spend on different types of marketing, based on what's working best for your competitors.

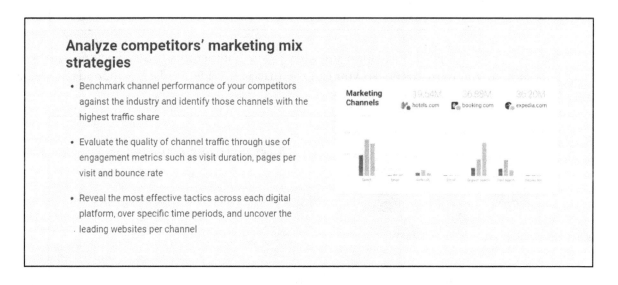

You can explore how well different keywords are working to draw traffic, so you can use the best ones on your website, in blogs, in advertising, in videos, and other materials.

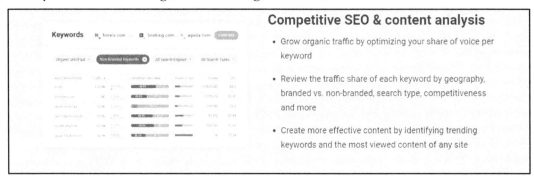

This marketing information can also help you assess how well affiliates are performing for you and your competitors by analyzing their traffic. Then, that can help you in selecting affiliates and in guiding them to perform better by sharing your insights about keywords and effective advertising.

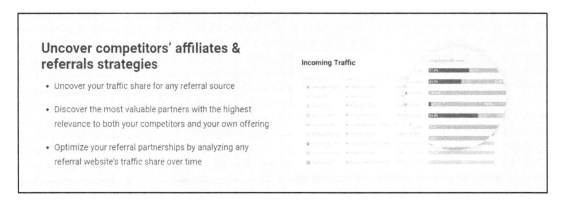

Then, too, you can get information on where your competitors are advertising and what advertising is drawing the most traffic, so you can use that as a guide to placing your ads as well as creating high-performing ad content.

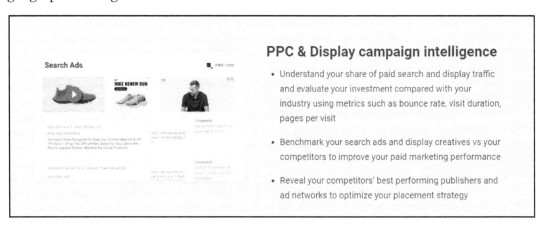

As the company describes, the main tools to understand the competition are Keyword Research and Analysis Tools; Referral and Affiliate Research Tools, Competitive Analysis Tools, and Media Buying and Creative Research Tools. In this way, you can get a comprehensive picture of your competitors' marketing mix and what strategies are working the best, so you can incorporate this information into your own marketing. By doing so, you will find yourself in good company with some of the biggest companies using these tools, such as Google, Walmart, and Adidas.

You can learn more from the company's library of articles on digital marketing, research, sales, conversion, and obtaining investors.

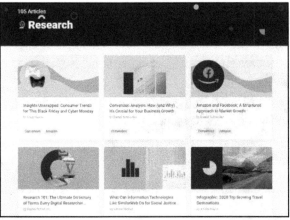

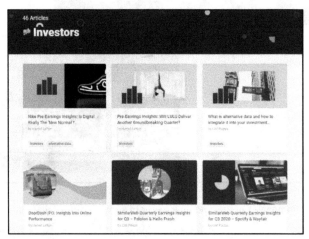

Plus there are all kinds of product guides on identifying industry trends, generating keywords, doing effective searches, learning about industry benchmarks and strategies, and more, so you can increase your knowledge about marketing methods generally, as well as use their search tools to learn more about particular competitors in your industry.

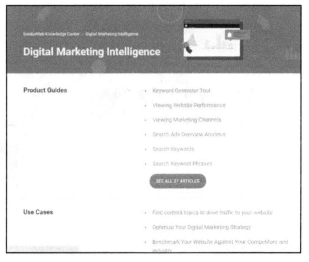

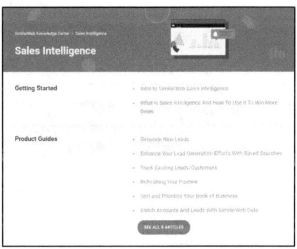

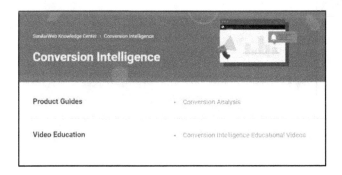

Additionally, the company offers numerous articles, blogs, and webinars about marketing strategies and other techniques to learn from your competitors and grow your business

How Does It All Work

Obtaining this kind of marketing data on competitors is not something you can do by yourself, given the extensive team used by Similar Web to gather the raw data about millions of companies and analyze this information. As this graphic illustrates, the company has over 500 staff members in four countries, and they have accessed 80 million websites to obtain data in 240 categories from 60 countries.

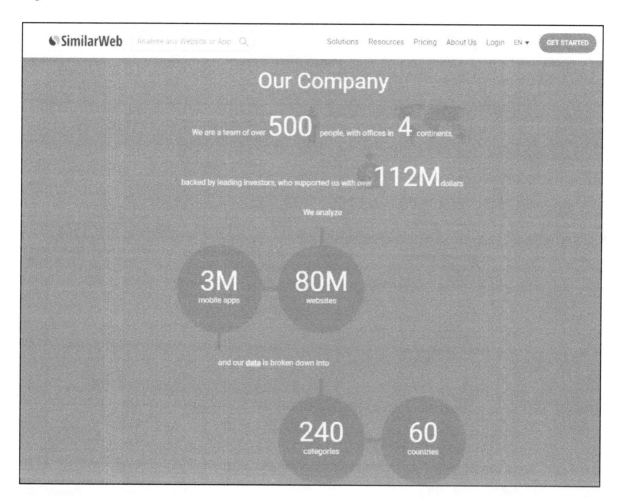

You can obtain three different types of data: keyword search information, display advertising insights, and information about referral partners. I'll describe each of these in turn.

Learning about Keywords

The goal of keyword research is to learn the most popular keywords, so you can incorporate them in your market efforts. Through this research, you can learn which top keywords produce the most traffic for your competitors and which keywords are new and trending. You can also discover the best keywords to use based on their search volume, click through rates, and the percentage of organic and paid clicks. Additionally, you can learn the trends in search traffic for different keywords.

For example, you can compare your company with one or two other companies or just see what other companies are doing. You can see how much traffic they are getting to their website, and you can compare the source of this traffic, such as what percent is coming from organic or paid ads and the amount of traffic based on their brand name.

You can also discover the level of traffic for yourself and your competitors for several months – such as from July to September, and compare how different companies are doing in getting traffic for organic and paid advertising, branded advertising, or for all types of ads. Such information can help you decide on how much of what type of advertising to use to best compete.

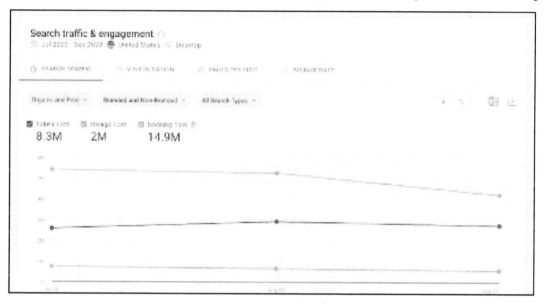

Another helpful insight is learning how well different keywords are pulling for organic and paid traffic and on mobile devices. This is also a way to recognize the different competitors attracting traffic with a particular keyword.

This keyword search can also reveal how long visitors stay on a page, how many other pages they visit, and the differences in the organic and paid traffic for a particular keyword.

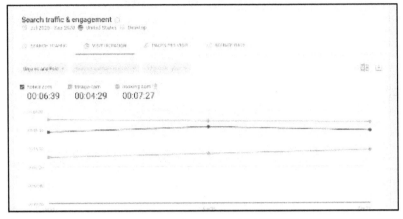

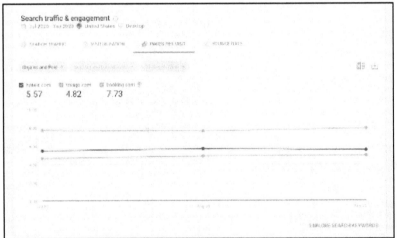

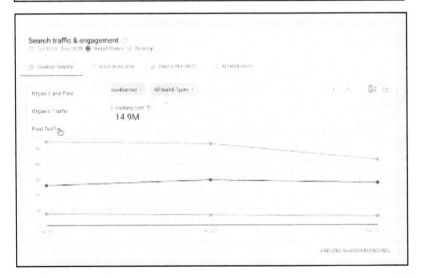

In addition, you can look more closely at the how well different keywords are performing for different competitors, and again make a comparison based on organic and paid traffic.

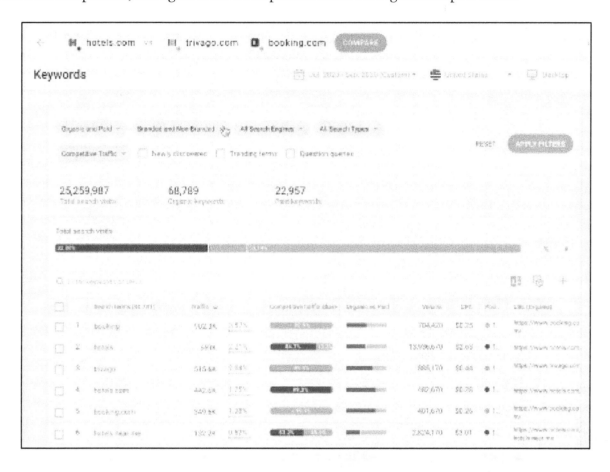

How do you know what keywords to use in comparing how well your competitors are doing with different keywords? You can look for keywords by entering keyword suggestions to find other keywords, or you can look by industry and compare the pulling power of different keywords for organic and paid traffic.

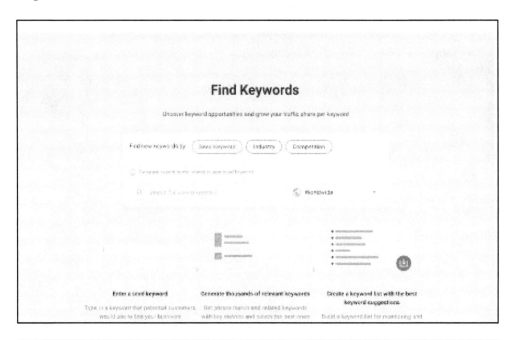

Then you can further drill down to learn the search volume for different keywords and the top sites attracting traffic with each keyword based on organic, paid, and mobile traffic. This search can also provide you with related phrases and keywords, so you can how well different keywords are doing for your competitors. Then, you can add the best performing keywords to your website and use them in your advertising.

To discover even more related and trending keywords, you can use a keyword generator. This process will also show you how well a keyword gets traffic for organic and paid advertising, as well and the company getting the most traffic using that word or phrase. To search for keywords just put the word or phrase in the search bar. Finally, create a named list for each keyword search.

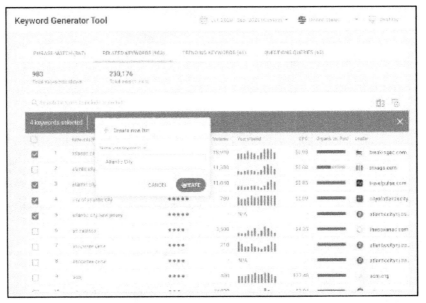

Learning about the Competitors' Advertising

Another thing to learn about your competitors is where they publish their ads and the type of advertising they use. For example, when you compare the traffic to the websites of three competitors, as in this comparison of Nike, Adidas, and a less well-known company, you can look at the number of ad visits and the relative amount of traffic they are getting from top publishers, including Facebook and from ad networks, including Google Display Ads.

You can see the total traffic they are getting, the length of the average visit, and the number of pages a visitor looks at.

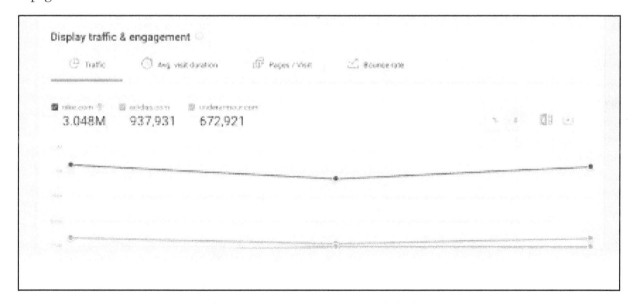

In addition, you can search for the top publishers your competitors are using by industry and see how they are doing with different publishers. These publishers include any publishing platform that features ads, including Facebook, YouTube, Yahoo, and a number of e-commerce sites.

Plus you can target the publishers or publishing platforms in different industries, such as in Fashion and Apparel, Beauty and Cosmetics, Gifts, Lifestyle Products, and more.

You can also examine how the advertising with different publishers has been performing in attracting visitors to your competitors' websites for both desktop and mobile users. This analysis will show you not only the total visits but the monthly visits by all visitors and by unique visitors, how long the visits last, and the number of pages visited.

You can also look at the number of visits from outgoing ads which are ads, which are the publishers' ads that go to other domains via referral links. In other words, you are assessing the amount of outgoing traffic from a publisher which is going to a paying advertiser or ad network.

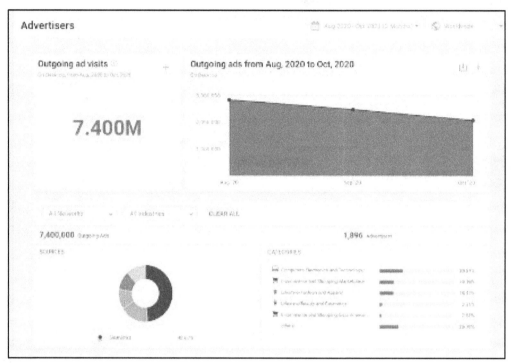

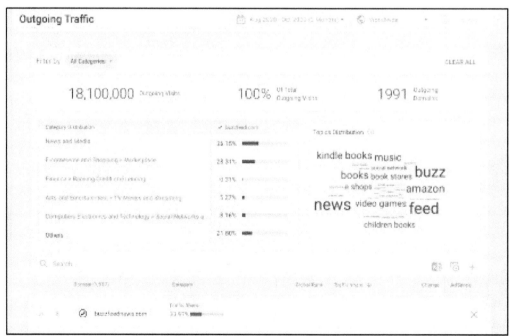

Additionally, you can also find and learn a company's display ads and from the videos on its website. You can learn from which ads are driving the most traffic and clicks, so you can use that approach in creating your own ads and videos. After that, you can see which of your ads and videos are driving the most traffic and double down on using the approach that works best.

Learning How Your Affiliates Are Doing

If you have affiliates marketing your products, you can use this platform to learn what they are doing on a daily, weekly, or monthly basis. You can see what advertising they are using and what kind of traffic they are generating. Then, that information can help you determine which affiliates are most effective, and you can help your affiliates do even better by advising them based on what you have learned about using keywords and ads to generate more traffic and sales.

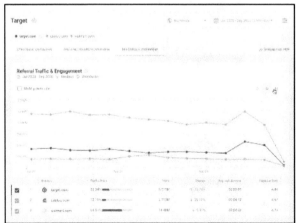

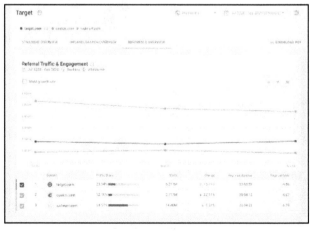

In conducting this referral analysis, you can look at your referral opportunities, including the number of websites sending visitors to your competitors' websites but not to yours. You can also discover your referral losses, which are the websites you or your affiliates are pursuing, but which you are losing to your competitors.

You can learn who are your most valuable referral sources, too.

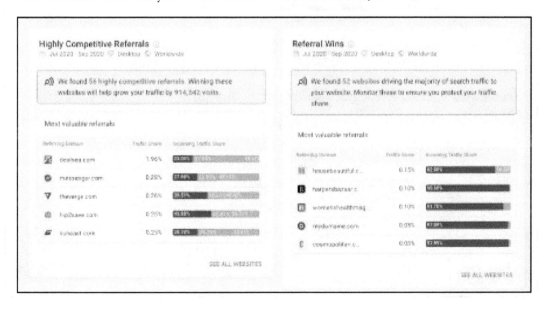

You can also assess the best referral websites by looking at the total referral visits each month during a selected time period, and you can compare how you are doing in different categories.

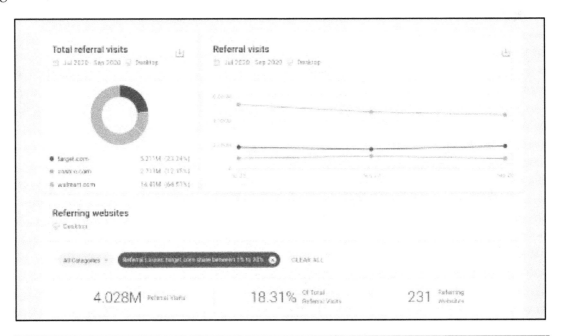

Finally, you can create customized partner lists, based on the partners performing the best.

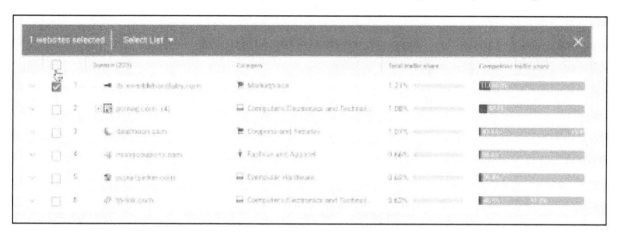

In sum, this platform can give you granular marketing intelligence about your competitors' traffic and the advertising used to generate this traffic. It can also help you assess the performance of any affiliates and help you advise them how they can do even better.

The key is learning what keywords, advertising, and publishing sources are working the best for you. While this platform attracts major companies with big budgets for marketing, you can also use it to gain marketing insights you can start applying, even if you only use the platform for a month or two.

As for pricing, there are various monthly and yearly plans, depending on what type of information you are looking for. You can try it out for free for one day, and then if you find it useful, you can opt for a plan focused on keywords (Search Marketing), on publishers and advertising (Display Marketing), and on referral information (Affiliate Marketing).

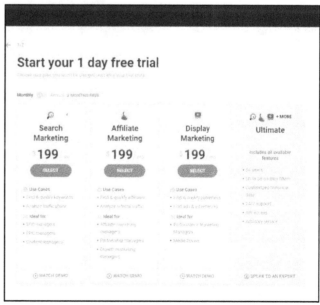

Given the depth of SimilarWeb's research on competitors, with their focus on keywords, publishing outlets, advertising, and affiliates providing referrals, it certainly seems like a worthwhile program if this information is useful for you. Also, the company has an extensive library of resources, articles, blogs, and webinars which can provide a comprehensive course on marketing strategy, should that be of interest.

CHAPTER 5: OTHER SOURCES OF INFORMATION ABOUT COMPETITORS

Still another way to learn about your competitors' advertising is enter a word or two characterizing your niche and the word "ad" in the search engine for the platform where you are considering advertising, In order to find competitor websites, you can do a search on Google for your category.

After you see the results, look more closely at the top ads. In some cases, you may get links to articles or groups interested in that topic, and you can check them out further. Some articles may provide examples of good ads in that category, and some may include the names of competitors and their websites.

You can learn more about the groups by going to their site, and sometimes you can join these groups, which might be a good source for promoting your product. However, take some time to learn what the group members are interested in and join the conversation before actively promoting your product, lest you be considered a spammer and possibly banned from the group.

To illustrate, here are the results from doing searches on Facebook and Google.

Finding Competitors' Ads on Facebook

Here are a few illustrations of finding competitors' ads on Facebook. To start, go to the "Search Facebook" link.

Say your category is "fitness," here are the top results for searching for "fitness ads".

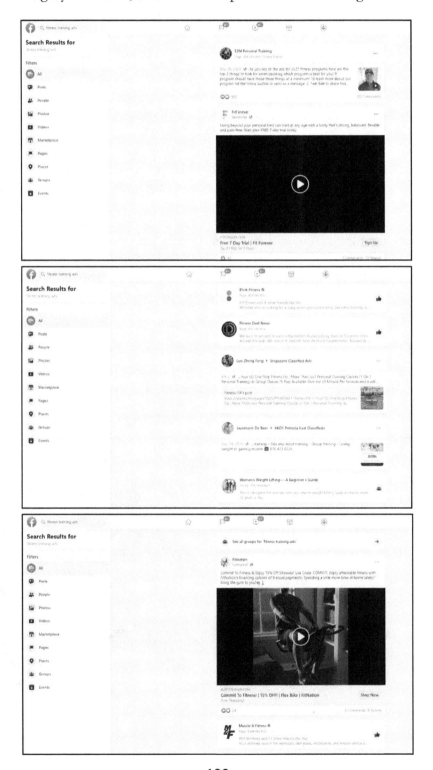

At the end of the listing of ads, you'll see some examples of related searches with similar names, such as for "fitness training," "fitness training videos," and "fitness training photos," so you can further search for more specific ads in your niche. Then, too, you might look for ads on related topics, such as "gym ads" and "physical exercise ads."

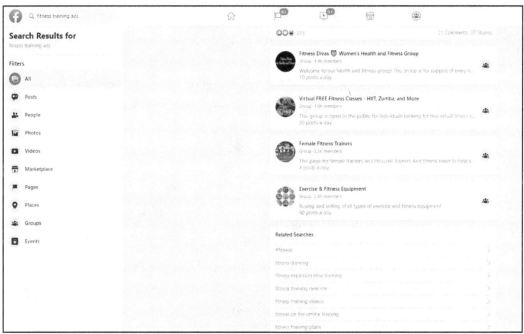

Here's another example for beauty products. As indicated in this example, sometimes the initial search term you enter, such as "beauty ads," brings up some unrelated topics, such as an ad with nothing to do with the subject or an ad about beauty in paintings rather than in products that improve one's beauty.

If the search does result in off-topic listings, put in more specific search terms, such as "beauty products ads." Once you do, the ads will be more on target.

Finding Competitors' Ads on Google

You can similarly search for competitors' ads on Google. For example, here is the first page of results, using the "fitness ads" term again. You'll first see the images for fitness ads, followed by several links from Google advertisers, some organic listings, and then some video ads.

Additionally, a Google search for "fitness ads" will reveal some top companies in this field.

You can follow these links to learn even more about the competitors in your field – from their websites to the advertising they are doing. As you explore these links, look for the keywords the companies are using on their websites and in their ads. Look at the copy, images, and videos clips. Later, you can use these ideas in creating or updating your website and determining how to feature your products on your website and in your ads.

Here's another example using the keyword "beauty" and the more specific "beauty products." In this case, the search term "beauty" triggers an ad for making ads for TikTok before showing images for beauty ads. Then, there are links to websites and articles, followed by suggestions for other searches

Here's an example of the results using the more specific "beauty products ads." In this case, the results are very similar, in contrast to getting more targeted results when using this term on Facebook. For example, there is the same sponsored listing for placing ads on TikTok, though the images for the beauty product ads are more targeted.

The links to articles in both searches are very similar, though the more targeted search results in more links to helpful articles, such as an article about successful Facebook ad campaigns for beauty products. Also, the suggestions about other beauty campaigns and ads are more specific.

Likewise, you can search on other platforms where you are considering advertising or want more information about your competitors, such as Instagram. Then, you can use this information to guide you in creating your own marketing strategies.

In some cases, you may find companies with related products that offer opportunities for advertising on their sides. Or you may find opportunities to enter into joint promotions and advertising with other companies in your space. Doing this research will give you insights and connections you can use in building your own brand and line of products.

ABOUT THE AUTHOR

GINI GRAHAM SCOTT, Ph.D., J.D., is a nationally known writer, consultant, speaker, and seminar leader, specializing in books on business, work relationships, professional and personal development, self-help, science, and crime. She has published over 50 books with major publishers. She has worked with dozens of clients on books and proposals on popular business, self-help, and memoirs, and has created book and script trailers for them. In addition, she writes film scripts and has produced 12 feature films, documentaries, and TV series. She writes the copy and works with a team of associates who help clients with social media posts, publicity, promotional videos, and web design.

She is the founder of Changemakers Publishing, featuring books on business, psychology, self-help, and social trends. The company has published over 200 print and e-books and over 150 audiobooks. She has licensed several dozen books for foreign sales, including the UK, Russia, Korea, Spain, and Japan. She has received national media exposure for her books, including appearances on *Good Morning America, Oprah,* and *CNN.*

Her books on marketing and sales include:
100 Ways to Gain More Success
How to Set Up Speaking Gigs and Get Paid
Increase Your Impact and Influence
Her books on work relationships and psychology include:
A Survival Guide for Working with Humans (AMACOM)
Lies and Liars: How and Why Sociopaths Lie (Skyhorse Publishing)
Her books on self-help include:
The Survive and Thrive Guide
What's Your Personality Type?
Her books on science and health include:
The Science of Living Longer: (Praeger) (and a documentary: *The New Age of Aging*)
The Very Next New Thing: (Praeger)
Her books on writing and self-publishing include:
How to Find and Work with a Good Ghostwriter
Self-Publishing Secrets and *Self-Publishing Your Book in Multiple Formats*
So You Want to Turn Your Book into a Film

Her films in distribution include *Driver* (Gravitas Ventures), Infidelity (Green Apple), *The New Age of Aging* (Factory Films) and *Me, My Dog and I* and *Rescue Me* (Random Media). The films are showcased at www.changemakersproductionsfilms.com.

Scott is active in several community and business groups, including the Lafayette Chamber of Commerce. She speaks on the topics of her books and on self-publishing. She received her PhD from the University of California, Berkeley, her JD from the University of San Francisco Law School, and five MAs at Cal State University, East Bay, most recently in Communication.

OTHER BOOKS BY THE AUTHOR

Other books by the author on business, marketing, sales, and self-help include:

100 Ways to Gain More Success
How to Set Up Speaking Gigs and Get Paid
Increase Your Impact and Influence
A Survival Guide for Working with Humans
Lies and Liars: How and Why Sociopaths Lie
The Survive and Thrive Guide
What's Your Personality Type?

CHANGEMAKERS PUBLISHING
3527 Mt. Diablo Blvd., #273
Lafayette, CA 94549
changemakers@pacbell.net . (925) 385-0608
www.changemakerspublishingandwriting.com

www.ingramcontent.com/pod-product-compliance
Lightning Source LLC
Chambersburg PA
CBHW082110070326
40689CB00052B/4371